The Jew's Harp

Karl Eulenstein, the great Jew's harp virtuoso, in 1833 at the age of thirty-one.

The Jew's Harp

A Comprehensive Anthology

SELECTED, EDITED, AND TRANSLATEI
BY

Leonard Fox

Lewisburg
Bucknell University Press
London and Toronto: Associated University Presses

Associated University Presses
440 Forsgate Drive
Cranbury, NJ 08512

Associated University Presses
25 Sicilian Avenue
London WC1A 2QH, England

Associated University Presses
P.O. Box 488, Port Credit
Mississauga, Ontario
Canada L5G 4M2

The paper used in this publication meets the requirements
of the American National Standard for Permanence of Paper
for Printed Library Materials Z39.48-1984.

Library of Congress Cataloging-in-Publication Data

The Jew's harp.

  Bibliography: p.
  Includes index.
  1. Jew's harp.   I. Fox, Leonard.
ML1087.J48   1988   788′.9   86-47991
ISBN 0–8387–5116–4 (alk. paper)

PRINTED IN THE UNITED STATES OF AMERICA

This anthology is dedicated to the memory of
Karl Eulenstein,
last and greatest virtuoso of the Jew's harp.
Er ruhe in Frieden.

Contents

Preface

"THERE IS SOMETHING about the Jew's harp that attracts more than usual affection for the instrument and everything about it. Other instruments have fans, enthusiasts, aficionados; the Jew's harp attracts zealots and fanatics. The explanation, I believe, is in the fact that the more irrational any behavior is, the more tenaciously one clings to it." So writes Professor Frederick Crane in the first issue of a periodical with the whimsical title, *Vierundzwanzigsteljahrsschrift der Internationalen Maultrommelvirtuosengenossenschaft* (Semimonthly Journal of the International Society of Jew's Harp Virtuosi), the only journal in the world devoted exclusively to all aspects of the Jew's harp.

My own involvement with the instrument began more than thirty years ago, at the moment when I spent a week's allowance to buy my first Jew's harp in the now long-defunct John Finster Music Shop on Lexington Avenue in New York City. I still have it—a wonderful Smith harp which, aside from a unique hand-forged Yakut instrument, is the best in my collection, attesting to the accuracy of statements by Scheibler and Schmidt in this anthology to the effect that Jew's harps improve with age.

As the years passed, my affection for the instrument grew, and I began to search for literature about it. My efforts were poorly rewarded, as almost nothing had been written about the Jew's harp in English. An extended stay in Germany yielded better results. I discovered the autobiography of Karl Eulenstein, perhaps the greatest Jew's harp virtuoso who ever lived, as well as several older articles which contributed significantly to knowledge of the instrument. Around this time, the magnificent catalogue of Jew's harps in the large collection of the Musée de l'Homme in Paris appeared, accompanied by invaluable scholarly and practical essays by Geneviève Dournon-Taurelle and John Wright. One major work which had eluded me after a five-year hunt in all the libraries of West and East Germany was finally found in a special collection of the New York Public Library's Music Division. This is Wilhelm Ludwig Schmidt's detailed manual, translated here after almost 150 years of relative oblivion.

The contents of this anthology have been selected on the basis of their intrinsic interest, their practical value to the would-be Jew's harp vir-

9

tuoso, and also for their rarity. For these reasons I have omitted such well-known articles as Curt Sachs's attempt at typology and descriptions of the oriental varieties of the Jew's harp. Information on typology, acoustics, the Jew's harp worldwide, and other topics has been included in the introduction; the notes to this and the extensive bibliography at the end of the book will provide readers with more detailed sources on these subjects. The notes to Karl Klier's article include a wealth of materials for those particularly interested in pursuing several aspects of the Jew's harp in Central Europe.

In reading this anthology, it will be noticed that both contradictions and repetitions occur among the various authors represented. The Jew's harp, unlike any other instrument (except perhaps that most ancient and venerated Chinese chordophone, the *ch'in*) has easily lent itself to my-thologizing; hence, the sometimes startingly contradictory information about it. In such cases, it is usually wisest to rely upon what may be termed the basic works—Scheibler, Schmidt, and Klier, as well as upon the synthetic study attempted in the introduction. Repetitions may be explained simply by the fact that because so very little has been written about the Jew's harp, the few fundamental works which exist are con-tinually quoted from—with or without attribution. Schmidt himself, as will be seen, plagiarizes quite shamelessly from Scheibler, although he acknowledges his debt to his older contemporary and mentor with such respectful and sincere eloquence that he may perhaps be forgiven for not bothering about precise source citations for some of his statements.

A word about the translations may be in order here. Every translator has his own philosophy about how faithful he need be in conveying a text from one language into another. My own feeling is that I would rather sacrifice a certain felicity of English phrasing to give the reader a close approximation of what he or she would experience by reading the author in German, French, or some other language. I believe that in reducing a variety of texts by different authors to the translator's own native language style, a blandness results which deprives the reader of an appreciation of the idiosyncratic nature of the originals.

Finally, after reading this book, the newly converted Jew's harp de-votee will wonder where to find good instruments. These are almost impossible to obtain in the United States, Canada, and England; but I have included at the end of this book two addresses at which they may be purchased.

Acknowledgments

I WISH TO THANK the following:

Bärenreiter Verlag, Kassel, Germany, for permission to translate Karl Klier's work, "Die Maultrommel," from *Volkstümliche Musikinstrumente in den Alpen*, 1956.

Ole Kai Ledang and the International Council for Traditional Music and its Secretary General, Dieter Christensen, for permission to quote extensively from Ole Kai Ledang's article, "On the Acoustics and the Systematic Classification of the Jew's Hårp," in *Yearbook of the International Folk Music Council, 1972*.

The Jew's Harp

Introduction

DESPITE THE GREAT intrinsic interest presented by many of its aspects—typological, historical, and acoustic, especially—the Jew's harp has attracted relatively little scholarly attention among musicologists, social historians, ethnologists, and acousticians. During the past 150 years, this lack of regard has perhaps been due in the West to the absence of recognized virtuosi whose mastery of the Jew's harp could have brought it to the notice of both the public and the specialist. As will be seen from the texts in this anthology, this was not always the case. During the period from approximately 1765, when the Austrian composer and organist Johann Georg Albrechtsberger was inspired to write a number of concerti for the Jew's harp, until about 1850, the instrument attained a remarkable prominence in the musical life of Western Europe. Through its leading exponents, particularly Koch, Kuhnert, and Eulenstein, it captivated such renowned individuals as the German writers Goethe, Schiller, and Jean-Paul Richter, as well as the English physicist and acoustician Charles Wheatstone. After this brief "golden age," however, the Jew's harp, for the most part, declined to the level of a folk instrument and, until recently, was more or less consigned to oblivion as far as serious scholarship is concerned.

Classification

Among the unresolved problems associated with the Jew's harp, that of its classification has occupied musicologists and acousticians for some time. The first mention of the instrument in this context was made by Sebastian Virdung, who grouped the Jew's harp together with rustic instruments, such as hunting horns, bird calls, and bells in his *Musica Getutscht* (Basel, 1511). About a century later, in *Theatrum Instrumentorum* (1618), Michael Praetorius classed the Jew's harp with the hurdy-gurdy, the viele, the horn, the triangle, and the bell. A far more precise approach to classification was made by the famous seventeenth-century musicologist Marin Mersenne (although he appears to have had two views on the matter): In *Traité des Instruments de Musique* (1640), Pierre Trichet states that Mersenne regarded the Jew's harp as a "pneumatic" instrument, since breath participated in producing its sounds, but that in the author's massive treatise *Harmonie Universelle* (1636), he termed it a chromatic or percussion instrument, because breath alone, without striking, does not make it yield any sound.

Modern attempts to classify the Jew's harp have still not settled the issue. Curt Sachs invented the term "plucked idiophone" for the instrument,[1] defining an idiophone as "an instrument which produces sounds due to the rigidity and elasticity of the material from which it is made, without the need for strings or a stretched membrane."[2] Most recently, Frederick Crane[3] and Ole Kai Ledang[4] have returned to Mersenne's original view and have classified the Jew's harp as an aerophone, essentially arguing that full functioning of the instrument occurs only when a stream of air moves past its tongue.

Although it seems that the classification decided upon by Crane and Ledang is the most satisfactory overall, it remains to future research to bridge the gap between a "plucked aerophone" and an idiophone which requires the presence of a stream of air.

Typology and Construction

The extended horseshoe- or bow-shaped instrument familiar to most people in the West is only one of two main types of Jew's harp, the other being a lamellate type in which the tongue of the instrument is cut through the frame. Curt Sachs, in his pioneering article on Jew's harp typology,[5] based his classification on the type of frame employed and, within that broad category, on whether the tongue was cut into the frame *(idioglot)* or whether it was attached to it *(heteroglot)*.

The schema that appears at the end of his article is as follows:

I. Frame Jew's harps [i.e., lamellate type—TRANS.]
   A. Idioglot Jew's harps
      1. Bamboo or wood Jew's harps
         a) Wedge-shaped tongue
         b) Graded tongue
            i) String
            ii) Handle
            iii) Thorn
         c) Blunt tongue
            i) String
            ii) Thorn-type end
         d) Tapered tongue
            i) String
            ii) Handle
            iii) Thorn-like tenon

    2. Sheet-metal Jew's harps
       a) Wedge-shaped tongue
       b) Tapered tongue
  B. Heteroglot Jew's harps
    1. Bamboo Jew's harps
    2. Metal Jew's harps
II. Bow-shaped Jew's harps
  A. With extended tongue
  B. Without extended tongue

Although Sachs obviously exercised extreme care in his schema, for some reason he neglected to list bone, horn, and mammoth ivory as materials to be found among the idioglot Jew's harps. These materials have been used extensively for lamellate Jew's harps among the native peoples of Siberia, in Mongolia, and by the Eskimo.

In an effort to reduce the complexity of Sachs's system and, at the same time, to indicate the method by which the Jew's harp actually functions during playing, Dournon-Taurelle and Wright[6] have proposed a classification based simply on whether the tongue of the instrument is enclosed within the frame or not, as they consider that many of the other criteria used by Sachs are of secondary relevance.

In general terms, the lamellate Jew's harp is a thin wooden, bamboo, bone, ivory, horn, or metal plate, measuring anywhere from about 8 to 35 centimeters in length, depending upon the culture of origin and the material employed. In the idioglot type, the tongue is cut lengthwise into the center of the plate and a string is sometimes attached to its base or to the base of the frame: by pulling the string, the player places the tongue in vibration. As Sachs indicates, the tongues may be of quite varied shape and, for ease of handling, a small thorn or wooden tenon is often tied to the end of the string. Some lamellate Jew's harps (among the Nepalese and the Lisu people of China, for example) have two or more tongues cut into them. In order to compensate for the very weak sounds produced by the lamellate Jew's harp, various types of resonators have been devised by cultures using this type of instrument: the Buang of New Guinea and the Javanese use a hollow bamboo tube, while the Balinese frequently place a sort of small fan behind the Jew's harp, which apparently changes the quality of the sound.

The bow-shaped Jew's harp is traditionally made of forged iron, although the cheaper modern instruments are either cast or, more usually, machine-formed from iron, aluminum, or alloy wire. Copper, brass, silver, and gold have also been used for the frames of this type of Jew's harp; but, in most cases, the tongue of the instrument, which is hammered or sometimes riveted into the frame, is made of tempered steel or—in Southeast Asia—of brass. Again, depending upon the culture of origin, bow-shaped Jew's harps range from approximately 5 to 15 centimeters in length. In those instruments (particularly from the Indian sub-continent) where the base of the tongue extends beyond the frame, the overall length may be considerable; indeed, there are some instruments where the length of the extension of the tongue is greater than the length of the frame itself. Resonators have also been used for this type of Jew's harp: some peoples of the Soviet Union use an axe-head for the purpose. In the United States, an instrument called the "Jewsaphone" was invented in the 1930s, consisting of a Jew's harp soldered to a small metal megaphone.

The most delicate part of the Jew's harp—whether lamellate or bow-shaped—is the tongue. Many cultures use some sort of protective device in order to ensure that this part of the instrument is not damaged or bent out of alignment, since the purity and strength of sound produced by a Jew's harp is contingent upon the smallest possible tolerance between the edges of the tongue and the inner sides of the frame between which it passes. In areas where bamboo lamellate Jew's harps are used, a hollow bamboo tube is used as a case for the instrument. In Siberia and other regions of the Soviet Union where wooden and metal lamellate types are played, the Jew's harp is often tied to a flat board and thereby suspended from the belt. Beautifully carved wooden cases, many of them in the form of shoes, were made in Europe, primarily in Austria and Norway, to protect the finely forged instruments.

Geographic Distribution

In one of its two forms, the Jew's harp is found as a native instrument throughout Europe, Asia, and the Pacific (except in Australia). Although lamellate bone and ivory Jew's harps are known among the Eskimo, no pre-Columbian traces of the instrument have been discovered in the Americas. Until it was introduced as a trade item by the Europeans, the Jew's harp was also unknown on the African continent. In the Soviet Union, it is found everywhere except in the Caucasus and in Karelia.[7]

It is not possible to draw lines of demarcation for the geographic distribution of the lamellate and bow-shaped types of Jew's harp. Basically, the bamboo and wooden lamellate types are found in the Pacific, in Southeast Asia, and in China (although the classical form of the Jew's harp in northern China is an iron idioglot lamellate instrument), while the metal bow-shaped type is much less widespread in these areas. The situation becomes far more complicated in the northern and central Asian regions, as well as on the Indian subcontinent. Here, the lamellate and bow-shaped types coexist extensively. In Siberia, for example, the Evenks have a bow-shaped metal instrument and a wooden lamellate one; the Udegei have a bow-shaped metal Jew's harp and a lamellate metal type; and the Nivkhs have three kinds—a bow-shaped iron instrument, a wooden lamellate one, and a copper lamellate one. Among some of these peoples, the bow-shaped type was used exclusively or primarily as a shamanist instrument, while the lamellate type was played in social contexts.[8] Among the Montagnard peoples of Laos and Vietnam, an unusual type of Jew's harp was developed, some examples of which have wooden frames and metal tongues; others are completely metal throughout, but in both cases, the tongue of the instrument, instead of being fixed or riveted at the base of the frame, is held in place by means of a fairly wide metal band.[9] In Europe, the bow-shaped metal type is the only kind of Jew's harp that has been discovered.

Through European colonization, the bow-shaped metal Jew's harp was introduced into the Americas, Africa, and Australia, as well as into many places where only the lamellate type had been known. In some areas of the Pacific, it supplanted the native lamellate instrument, as it was superior in volume and resonance. Jew's harps were among the early trade items brought by the Dutch and English to North America, and the instruments have been unearthed in excavations of Native American village sites. The Jew's harp achieved great popularity in sub-Saharan Africa and, to a lesser extent, in Madagascar, where a well-developed musical tradition, using native instruments, was already established. The Maori of New Zealand received Jew's harps from the English with great enthusiasm; the instruments were accepted in early payments for land.[10]

Methods of Playing

Depending upon the type of Jew's harp employed, there are three ways of placing the tongue of the instrument in vibration: plucking, striking, and traction. Plucking is used with bow-shaped Jew's harps, where the free end of the tongue is plucked either with a finger of the same hand that holds the instrument or with one finger of the other hand; and, with lamellate Jew's harps, where either the extension of the tongue is plucked or, in the absence of this, the end of the frame itself. Some lamellate Jew's harps, especially in New Guinea, are held in one hand and the tongue is struck at a certain point against the wrist of the other hand or, in the case of some Javanese instruments, for example, the end of the frame is struck with a finger of the hand that is not holding the Jew's harp. Traction is used with many lamellate Jew's harps: a string, attached either to the base of the frame or to the tongue itself, is pulled sharply and then immediately released. The traction method of playing is distributed throughout the Indonesian archipelago, as well as in India, Nepal, Burma, Tibet, and China, among the Siberian peoples, the Ainu of northern Japan, and the Eskimo. It is often found coexisting with the plucking method—quite obviously where bow-shaped Jew's harps are also used—and, much more rarely, with the striking method.

Since the basic theme of this anthology is the Jew's harp in Western Europe, the following description of playing method relates to the bow-shaped metal Jew's harps most commonly encountered in Europe and the Americas. Right-handed players grasp the instrument in the left hand, usually placing the thumb at the point on the outside of the frame where the tongue is joined to it, and the index and middle fingers at the points where the two extended parallel arms of the frame meet the rounded part. The instrument is brought to the mouth and the frame arms are held against the front teeth, which are opened slightly. The lips are positioned is such a way as to enclose partially the arms of the frame, but not to interfere with the free movement of the instrument's tongue. Sounds are produced by simultaneously breathing, plucking the upright end of the tongue, and varying the size of the oral cavity. Essentially, the technique involved in the last is the same as that used in whistling: the more volume permitted to the oral cavity, the lower the note produced, the less volume, the higher the note.

Although most players today are content to use only one Jew's harp at a time (albeit, some instruments with two tongues are still made), it was a common practice in the Tyrol, up to the 1920s, for good musicians to play two Jew's harps at the same time, holding one in each hand, usually with the thumb, index and ring fingers, while plucking with the middle finger. The instruments were tuned a fourth or a fifth apart, so that very attractive harmonies could be produced. This technique was also employed by all the great virtuosi of the eighteenth and nineteenth centuries, most of whom would play at a table on which were ranged large numbers of Jew's harps in various keys (Karl Eulenstein, for example, used sixteen of them). In the playing of complex pieces of music, they would very rapidly change instruments without interrupting the music. A few players used the Aura, an invention of Heinrich Scheibler, which combined up to ten differently tuned Jew's harps on a circular plate. Holding one plate in each hand, they thus had access to twenty instruments. The techniques involved in using this composite instrument are described at length in the present anthology.

Among non-Western peoples, the Na-khi people of Yunnan province in China are known to have used three small lamellate Jew's harps, ranged one above the other, simultaneously.[11] The Altays of the Soviet Union are surely unique in their method of playing the Jew's harp:

expert performers hold the instrument in their mouths and set its tongue in motion with their own tongues![12]

Refinements of Jew's harp playing techniques have developed in many cultures. These include various types of tonguings to produce staccato and trill effects, strong and weak breathing to vary the volume and quality of the sounds, raising the back of the tongue to the soft palate in order to compensate for notes which are lacking due to the tuning of the instrument, combining the whispered utterance of words or syllables with other means of sound production, birdsong effects, and so forth. In Romania, small tuning slides are sometimes fitted over the tongues of Jew's harps to change the pitch, while tiny balls of sealing wax or shellac have been used for tuning the instrument of Western Europe.

Acoustics

The first scientific investigations of Jew's harp acoustics were made in the ninteenth century by Gottfried Weber,[13] Charles Wheatstone,[14] and Wilhelm Weber.[15] All three writers concluded that the production of harmonics on the fundamental frequency of the instrument's tongue was made by changes in the volume of the oral cavity and not by the Jew's harp itself. It was only in 1967 that Emile Leipp disproved this hypothesis by means of spectral analysis and showed that in and of itself the Jew's harp produces a wide harmonic spectrum without the presence of a resonator.[16] In playing, therefore, the oral cavity simply modifies the inherent harmonic capabilities of the instrument.

Based upon Leipp's research and his own extensive knowledge of the construction and playing of the Jew's harp, Ole Kai Ledang carried out a number of experiments and determined that the sound spectrum produced by any given Jew's harp is based not only on the vibration of the tongue, but also on the degree of tolerance between the edges of the tongue and the inner sides of the parallel arms of the Jew's harp frame.[17] He proved this contention by constructing an experimental Jew's harp, the parallel arms of which could be adjusted for distance from the tongue. Ledang formulated his conclusions as follows:

> The transverse vibration of the lamella [i.e., the tongue] approximates a harmonic motion, corresponding to the first resonant frequency of the lamella. Consequently, the spectrum emitted by the lamella alone has a very predominant fundamental and compatatively weak overtones. However, when vibrating vigorously between the sharp edges of the parallel arms of the frame, the lamella creates turbulence in the surrounding air. *Due to this turbulence in the surrounding air, a harmonic sound spectrum is generated and emitted,* the fundamental frequency of which corresponds to the fundamental frequency of

the lamella. (The harmonic partials of the spectrum emitted by the lamella alone also must be ascribed to turbulence in the surrounding air.)

This explains why, on some jaw's harps, the inner edges of the arms (as well as both edges of the lamella) are often made as sharp as possible in order to make the instrument sound well. This kind of preparation has to do with the formation of turbulence, which is thereby favored. Further, the phenomenon of turbulence occurs quite independent of the material from which the instrument is made, furnishing thus the general acoustical principle, by which the homogeneity in sound quality of different types of jaw's harps may be explained. It should be noted that the turbulence—and with it, the harmonic spectrum—arises whether there is an air-stream moving past the lamella or not. According to this, the breathing of the player cannot be considered essential to the sound-producing mechanism of the instrument. However, by means of breathing, the player may influence to a certain degree the process of sound generation from the jaw's harp during playing, and thus modulate the musical sound in a subtle manner.[18]

History and Use

Another unresolved series of problems presented by the Jew's harp relates to its historical development and the cross-cultural contacts involved in its geographic distribution. Although it seems evident that the Jew's harp is an extremely ancient instrument, the rapidly decomposable nature of the materials from which most of the lamellate types are made precludes the discovery of any older examples. Soviet scholarship has as yet provided no information on the dating of bone instruments from Siberia.

In very broad terms it may be said that, aside from differences in the shape and extension of the tongue, lamellate Jew's harps from Asia and the Indonesian archipelago display a great degree of uniformity in that the tongues are cut directly through the frame, leaving the ends of the frame a solid whole. In New Guinea and the Solomon Islands, on the other hand, the end of the frame is split or cut and the cut is continued on two sides to form the tongue; the split end of the frame is left open in some examples and tied together in others.[19] (For a full discussion of the construction of both lamellate and bow-shaped Jew's harps, see Dournon-Taurelle and Wright, 45–55 and 97–101.)

Despite the fact that there is no specific evidence to support the hypothesis, it appears likely that the lamellate type of Jew's harp is the older form. As mentioned above, among some peoples such as the Maori, the introduction of European metal Jew's harps almost entirely displaced the use of the earlier bamboo or wooden instruments, while among others, the lamellate and bow-shaped types continued to coexist. It is perhaps indicative of the great age of the Jew's harp, as well as of the musical conservatism of the cultures of Indonesia, that although an extensive and highly developed group of metal percussion instruments have been in use in the area for hundreds of years, few attempts have been made to construct metal Jew's harps. In addition, the introduction of European instruments by the Dutch has apparently had little significant impact on their former colonies in the East Indies.

With regard to Indonesia, one puzzling phenomenon should be mentioned. Most scholars agree on the fact that Madagascar was settled by successive migrations of a people originating in the Indonesian archipelago, the last wave of which may have occurred as late as the fourteenth century. Linguistic evidence seems to indicate the island of Borneo as the most likely point of origin.[20] The Jew's harp, however, appears to have been unknown in Madagascar until its introduction by the English, although the instrument is used in Borneo, and the Merina tribe, the last immigrants from Indonesia to Madagascar, play an instrument called the *valiha*—a sort of upright tubular bamboo zither—which is almost identical to instruments found in Vietnam, the Philippines, and in many places in Indonesia.

In Europe, the oldest Jew's harps so far discovered are a group of five bronze instruments dating from the Gallo-Roman period, found in Rouen in 1868. In form, they very closely resemble instruments made up to the present time and are especially similar to the type of Jew's harp— with a relatively small rounded portion of the frame and long parallel arms—commonly forged in Norway until a few years ago. An instrument of the same type was found in the ruins of the Tannenberg fortress in Germany, destroyed in 1399. Twelfth- and thirteenth-century Jew's harps have been discovered in Switzerland and several instruments dating from the fourteenth and fifteenth centuries have been found in Sweden and Romania. Although the tongues of these Jew's harps have decayed with time, the extant remnants of the earliest ones indicate that they extended beyond the base of the frame. This fact and the general shape of the frame led Curt Sachs to conclude that the Asian type of bow-shaped Jew's harp was the direct ancestor of the European instrument, inasmuch as Jew's harps of precisely this kind are still in wide use, especially in India, Nepal, and Afghanistan.[21]

Little is known of the status of the Jew's harp during the Middle Ages, but graphic representations of the instrument during this period would seem to indicate that in addition to its use by the peasant population, it was also played by professional musicians. One of the stone sculptures of the cathedral at Exeter, England, portrays an angel playing the Jew's harp, and in a painting of the Virgin and Child from the late medieval period, three angels are shown in the background: one is playing a Jew's harp, one a tromba marina, and one a fiddle. This would appear to demonstrate that before the seventeenth century, the Jew's harp was accorded a somewhat more exalted place in the hierarchy of musical instruments than that to which it was relegated by Marin Mersenne, who declared it to be an instrument of lackeys and people of the lower classes.[22]

The fact that about one hundred years after the publication of Mersenne's magnum opus, the Benedictine monk Father Bruno Glatzl was widely renowned for his mastery of the Jew's harp may indicate that a certain virtuoso tradition of Jew's harp playing still continued—at least in Germany and Austria—and that Mersenne's generalization was perhaps a bit too sweeping. The most obvious evidence of this is to be found in the records of a concert given in Nürnberg in 1643, at which several Jew's harps were also played. Jew's harps were, in fact, reputedly used in court orchestras during the seventeenth and eighteenth centuries.[23]

The seventeenth century also witnessed an increased demand for Jew's harps throughout Europe. In order to satisfy this demand, a group of smiths in the town of Molln, in the Austrian region of Steyr, formed a guild of Jew's harp makers, which survived at least until 1925. Eventually, Jew's harps were exported from Molln to every continent and the town remains the world center of Jew's harp manufacture to the present day.

In 1764, the Austrian composer and teacher of Beethoven, Johann Georg Albrechtsberger, was present at a concert given by Father Bruno Glatzl in the Benedictine monastery of Melk in honor of the Emperor Josef II, who was returning from his coronation in Frankfurt. Albrechtsberger was then organist at the monastery, but after moving to Vienna, the deep impression made upon him by Father Glatzl's virtuoso performance inspired him to write at least seven concerti for Jew's harp, mandora (a kind of small, eight-course lute), and strings, three of which—composed in 1769, 1770, and 1771—have survived in the Esterhazy collection, now part of the National Széchényi Library in Budapest. With the composition of Albrechtsberger's concerti, the golden age of the Jew's harp had begun.

After Father Glatzl, the next great virtuoso of the instrument to appear was Franz Koch. Biographical data on this remarkable performer appear elsewhere in this anthology, but it was undoubtedly Jean-Paul Richter who first brought Koch to the notice of the literary world of the late eighteenth and early nineteenth centuries. In his novel, *Hesperus, oder fünfundvierzig Hundsposttage* [*Hesperus, or Forty-Five Dog-Post-Days*], which enjoyed tremendous popularity after its appearance in 1795, the author mentions Koch by name and introduces him into the action of the book by describing a private concert given by the musician:

The name of Franz Koch in the Dog's papers made me jump off my feet. If any one of my readers is a guest of the Carlsbad waters, or should happen to be his Majesty, the King of Prussia, William the Second, or one of his court, or the elector of Saxony, or the Duke of Brunswick, or any other princely person, he has heard the good Koch, who is a modest pensioned soldier, and travels round everywhere with his instrument and plays on it. This instrument, which he calls the double Jews-harp or mouth-harmonica, consists of an improved pair of jaw-drums [a more or less literal translation of the German term for the Jew's harp, *Maultrommel*—Ed.] or humming jaws-harps played at once, which he shifts according to the piece he is playing. His handling of the buzzing-irons bears the same relation to the old Jews-harp playing as harmonica-bells do to servants' bells. I am under obligation to induce such of my readers as have wren's wings to their fancy, or at least, from the heart upwards are *lithopaedia* (petrified foetuses), or have the ear-drum membrane for nothing but to be drummed on, —to induce, I say, with the little oratory I have, such readers to tumble the aforesaid Franz out of the house, if he undertakes to come and buzz before them. For it amounts to just nothing, and the wretchedest bass-viol or rebeck screams louder in my opinion; nay, its hum is so low, that he played at Carlsbad before not more than twelve customers at once, because one cannot sit near enough to him, particularly as in his leading pieces he has the light carried away, that neither eye nor ear may disturb the fantasies. If, however, a reader is differently constituted—a poet, perchance, —or a lover, —or very tender, —or like Victor, —or like me; then, indeed, let him without scruple listen with still and melting soul to Franz Koch, or—for to-day is just the time when he is not to be had—to *me*.

The jolly Englishman had sent this harmonist to Victor with the card: "The bearer of this is the bearer of an echo which he carries in his pocket . . ."

[Clotilda] begged her father, who had already heard the mouth-harmonica in Carlsbad, to give her and Victor an idea of it, —he gave it: "It expressed in masterly manner not so much the *fortissimo* as the *piano-dolce*, and, like the simple harmonica, was best adapted to the *adagio*."

. . . But scarcely had the modest, quiet virtuoso put the instrument of enchantment to his lips, when Victor felt that now (before the light was removed) he should not dare to do as at other times, when he pictured to himself at every adagio appropriate scenes, and underlaid every piece with peculiar fantasyings for its texts. For it is an unfailing method of giving tones their omnipotence, when one makes them the accompanying voices of our inner mood, and so out of instrumental music makes as it were vocal music, out of inarticulate tones articulate ones, whereas the fairest series of tones, which no definite subject arranges into alphabet and speech, glides off from bathed, but not softened, hearts. When, therefore, the sweetest sounds that ever flowed over human lips as consonants of the soul began to well forth from the trembling mouth-harmonica, —when he felt that these little steel-rings, as if they were the setting and touch-board of his heart, would make their agitations his own, then did he constrain his feverish heart, on which, besides, all wounds came out to-day, to shrink up against the tones, and not picture to himself any scenes, merely that he might not burst into tears before the light was gone.

But the light was just then carried from the chamber, and the first stream fell unseen into the lap of night.

The harmonica began the melody of the dead: "How softly they slumber." Ah, in such tones do the far-wandering waves of the sea of eternity beat against the hearts of darkling mortals who stand on the shore and yearn to put forth!

. . . The tune stopped and died away. What stillness now in the dark! Every sigh took the form of a long-drawn breathing. Only the nebulous stars of sensibility sparkled in the darkness. No one saw whose eye had been wet. Victor looked into the still, black air before him, which a few minutes ago had been filled with hanging-gardens of tones, with dissolving air-castles of the human ear, with diminished heavens, and which now remained a naked, black firework-scaffold.

But the harmonica soon filled this darkness again with meterological apparitions of worlds. . . .

Finally, only the last lingering tone of the song still flung out its melodious circles in the ether, and its wake undulated away over a whole past, —then a distant echo wrapped it up in a fluttering breath of air, and wafted it away through deeper echoes, and finally over to the last which lay round about heaven, —then the tone expired and flew as a soul into one of Clotilda's sighs.[24]

Several years before the publication of *Hesperus*, Christian F. D. Schubart had written, probably with Koch in mind: "Sonatas, variations and all sorts of pieces are now played on the Jew's harp. It has even been found that the resonance of this most disdained instrument is among the most delicate tones in the world."[25]

By 1831, the year of Koch's death, the finest and most famous of the European Jew's harp virtuosi had already made careers for themselves with the instrument. About some of these individuals we know little more than what Wilhem Ludwig Schmidt included in his remarkable treatise on the Jew's harp, which was issued in 1840. A few of them were amateurs of the instrument, but excellent performers nonetheless. Heinrich Scheibler, the inventor of the Aura, for example, was a wealthy silk manufacturer, but his playing on the instrument he himself devised was recalled in the following terms by the poet Hofmann von Fallersleben, who had heard him in Dusseldorf in 1821: "His wonderful playing on the mouth-harmonica has remained unforgettable for me. These were tones which resounded from another world, like a secret magic which penetrated deep into the soul."[26]

Dr. Michael Kosmeli (1773–1844) was not only a well known Jew's harp virtuoso, but a polymath of astounding achievements. He studied both law and medicine, was a remarkable linguist and art connoisseur, a geographer and natural scientist, and a poet and prose writer. He played several musical instruments, but was most distinguished for his abilities on the Jew's harp. He was an untiring traveler and, in addition to Jew's harp concerts in several German cities, he performed on the instrument in numerous cities of the Russian empire, including Moscow, St. Petersburg, and Riga. Kosmeli was also important as the inspiration and teacher of Schmidt, whose book on the Jew's harp—the most complete work on the instrument until now—is included in this anthology.[27]

Schmidt (1787–1858) was trained as a medical doctor and practiced during his lifetime in several German cities. Interested in music from an early age, he had heard Koch play the Jew's harp, but as he himself says, it was Kosmeli who provided the impetus for him to master the instrument and who also gave him personal instruction in playing. It is unlikely that Schmidt ever gave public concerts, as there are no contemporary accounts of any, nor does he mention the fact in his book, but he was undoubtedly a highly competent performer on the Jew's harp in the form of the Aura, the use of which he endeavored to promote, albeit, without any noticeable success.

Both Schmidt and Eulenstein are lavish in their praise of the Bohemian Jew's harp virtuoso Friedrich Kuhnert, who, for nine years, gave concerts on the Jew's harp as a peripatetic musician throughout Germany and in Vienna. Judging by the reviews which appeared occasionally in the *Allgemeine musikalische Zeitung*, Kuhnert's playing was exceptionally fine and he, like Eulenstein, used a range of sixteen tuned Jew's harps in his performances. Karl Klier writes in his article (see page 69) that Kuhnert was Eulenstein's teacher, but this is not so; rather, Eulenstein may have used Kuhnert's playing as a model and an inspiration to develop his own technique.

We are extremely fortunate to possess the autobiography of Karl Eulenstein, who, by all accounts, must be considered the greatest of all the Jew's harp virtuosi. There are few documents of this type which give such an intimate portrayal of the hardships and almost incredible tenacity involved in the production of a finished artist, particularly one who was almost entirely self-taught. Contemporary reviews of Eulenstein's playing, some of which were prefaced by his daughter in her edition of the autobiography, indicate that not only did the brilliant execution of the music astound audiences and critics alike, but the very quality of the sounds which Eulenstein managed to elicit from the instrument were unlike anything that had ever been heard before. Eulenstein, like the other nineteenth-century masters of the Jew's harp (with the technical exception of Kosmeli), had no students. His art, therefore, has been permanently lost and the features of musical genius which characterized the uniqueness of his playing can only be imagined.

Although Eulenstein died in 1890, at the age of 88, he was obliged to stop playing the Jew's harp in 1834, due to severe problems with his teeth. Schmidt mentions one or two other virtuosi who were probably active at the time his book was published (1840), but it is fairly certain that after 1850 there were no longer any professional musicians who gave Jew's harp concerts. The instrument remained in the hands of folk music performers, some of whom, however, were very expert players, although their technical skill was on a totally different level from that of the virtuosi. The last well-known individual in the music world to have played the Jew's harp was the Austrian composer Hugo Wolf, who had learned the instrument in his youth.[28] Regrettably, he never composed any music for it.

Aside from its social use as a musical instrument, the Jew's harp, as Schmidt mentions, was also employed therapeutically in the nineteenth century. Aside from Schmidt himself, who describes the medical effects of his playing, perhaps the most famous exponent of its healing properties was Dr. Friedrich Mesmer, who utilized the gentle sounds of the instrument in his early experiments in psychotherapy. Eulenstein's first patron, the writer Justinus Kerner, a great admirer of the Jew's harp and himself an amateur performer on it, mentions the instrument in this context in his *Seherin von Prevost* [Seeress of Prevost] (1829): "Through the tones of this instrument, the terrible cramp left her immediately and she emerged from it in a healed state."

This application of the Jew's harp resembles in a strangely close manner its employment in shamanist rituals among the peoples of Siberia and Mongolia, where it was used both to induce trance and to heal the sick. As employed among the Darkhat shamans of northern Mongolia, there are three methods of playing:

> *shuud tsokhilt* ("direct stroke") is a regular rhythmic stroke with no change of pitch, symbolizing the journey along a road; *khelnii tsokhilt* ("tongue stroke"), made by moving the tongue back and forth to create different pitches, is used to imitate the cries of animals and to communicate with animal spirits; and *ongodiin tsokhilt* ("spirit stroke") imitates the trotting of an animal and is used when the spirit is believed to have left the body of the shaman and to be returning to its home in the tent or in the mountains and rivers.[29]

As a folk instrument, the Jew's harp was used extensively throughout Europe and North America. Its low cost made it accessible to almost everyone and it was played widely to accompany both dance and song. Swiss records as early as the sixteenth century note its use to accompany dancing. It was mentioned in eighteenth- and nineteenth-century Russian sources as "an instrument of the common people," but it appears to have lost its popularity almost completely in Russia itself by the beginning of the twentieth century, due to the increasing prevalence of the accordion, which was responsible for the demise of other folk instruments as well. It has continued to be used, however, in other European parts of the Soviet Union, especially in the Carpathian region of the Ukraine, and in Moldavia, where there are still some highly accomplished performers. Norway, Sardinia, Sicily, and the Tyrol have all been centers of Jew's harp playing for centuries. Many exceptionally fine instruments have been forged in these places and, in Norway, at least, there has been growing interest among young craftsmen in reviving the art of Jew's harp making, since the death of the last traditional artisan, Knut Gjermundsson Hovet, several years ago.

In North America, Jew's harps were brought by the first colonists and the instruments began to be manufactured in 1650 in Massachusetts.[30] Jew's harps have been discovered at Revolutionary War sites, as well as at other seventeenth- and eighteenth-century sites along the whole eastern seaboard. As already stated, the instruments were used extensively in trade with the Native Americans and thus are found at every point and in every period of westward expansion.

Among the uses to which the Jew's harp has been put, there is one which has a remarkable universality. The instrument has been employed in courting practices in such disparate places as Austria, Siberia, China, Cambodia, Indonesia, the Philippines, New Zealand, and New Guinea, among others. Klier quotes the saying current in Tyrol at the time of his field research that "A woman will do anything because of a Jew's harp." So far, there have been no psychosexual analyses of the Jew's harp, but in form the instrument represents quite graphically the union of male and female genitalia, as depicted in drawings and paintings from paleolithic times to the present, either in connection with fertility rites or—in the case of the Tantric art of Hinduism and Buddhism—in religious contexts. As a sort of three-dimensional archetypal image of sexual union, therefore, it is perhaps not unusual that the Jew's harp has been and continues to be closely connected with formal courtship.

On the other hand, it should also be mentioned that in many cultures, especially among the Turkic peoples of Central Asia, the Jew's harp is played exclusively or primarily by women and children. Alternatively, the non-metallic lamellate types are played by women and the bow-shaped iron type by men. The sexual associations of the instrument thus promise to be an interesting and fruitful area for future research.

Related to and often involved in its employment in courting is the use of the Jew's harp together with speech. In the southern Philippines, boys and girls carry on "conversations" while playing the instrument and these exchanges are considered to be incomprehensible to their parents; the same is true among the Lihjiang Moso people of China. Similar practices are found in New Guinea and were also noted by early travelers among the Maori. The Ket of Siberia actually tell stories while playing the Jew's harp and the Yakuts have developed a distinct style of playing called "talking Jew's harp."

Manufacture

Details of the manufacturing methods formerly used in Riva and in Molln—a small town in Austria which has been the center of Jew's harp production in Western Europe for almost 400 years—are to be found elsewhere in this anthology. At the present time, there is only one family in Austria whose members still make Jew's harps entirely by hand for limited commercial distribution in Europe; small numbers of these instruments are imported into the United States. Otherwise, all the Jew's harps currently made in Molln are manufactured by machine, with a consequent and regrettable loss in quality of resonance and sound production. The largest firm involved in this trade is that of Schwartz: their yearly production ranges between 270,000 and 350,000 instruments, which are exported to nineteen countries, including the United States.[31]

In other areas of the world, however, it has usually been the village blacksmith who has made Jew's harps for local musicians. This tradition died out only recently in rural Norway and is still alive in Sardinia and Sicily. In the USSR, there are still one or two blacksmiths among the Yakut of Siberia who forge and finish Jew's harps according to ancient, highly effective methods. These include literally tailor-making the instrument to fit the player. A musician who wants to have a Jew's harp made goes to stay with the smith for up to several days, during which time the latter studies his voice, breathing, hands, mouth formation, and teeth. Only then does the artisan feel able to forge a suitable instrument. This in itself is a lengthy process, involving a complex form of tempering called *metekel*. Included in this procedure are such substances as water, fish oil, sour cream, and the powdered horn of an adult bull.[32]

Jew's harps were widely manufactured in Great Britain in the nineteenth century, although the market for British instruments was smaller than that for the Austrian ones. Many of the former were cast, rather than forged or formed from heavy wire, which affected the tone adversely. The last family firm to produce Jew's harps—that of Trowman—closed in 1945, but instruments, mostly of very poor quality, are still being made in England.

Some of the finest Jew's harps produced commercially in this century were made in the United States by the Smith brothers of Rensselaer, New York, who were active from the 1930s until about 1965. Their early pattern, which was made in a large and a small size, was very beautiful and had slight indentations at the two points on the frame where the instrument is held by the index and middle fingers; the parallel arms of the frame were tapered and the steel tongue was well tempered, sharpened on the edges and precisely fitted to yield the narrowest possible tolerance between it and the frame arms. These instruments were apparently too costly to produce in large quantities and the Smiths later settled on a lyre-shaped pattern, which was also extremely well made. After their retirement, Tom Bilyeu, whose workshop is in Molalla, Oregon, purchased the Smiths' pattern and has been producing instruments of good quality ever since. He has recently been experimenting with a Jew's harp in which the tongue is attached to the frame by two small screws, so that it can be replaced, if broken or damaged. Fred Whitlow, of Palmetto, Florida, has been making some very fine Jew's harps on the later Smith model, which are available tuned in various keys, while A. J. Wininger, of Gate City, Virginia, has devised an unusual and attractive Jew's harp which he makes out of heavy copper wire. These two craftsmen make all of their instruments by hand and thus are not equipped to produce commercial quantities.

One of the most important considerations in the manufacture of Jew's harps is that the iron frame should be left unpainted or unplated, as any sort of coating tends to dull the sound of the instrument. Unfortunately, the Austrian firms whose instruments are most widely available tend to use both plating and paint, which they obviously feel improve the appearance of the Jew's harps. This fact and the excessively wide tolerance between tongue and frame arms unfortunately make most of the commercially manufactured instruments relatively unplayable. The very great decline in the quality of readily available Jew's harps over the last twenty-five years or more has undoubtedly been partly responsible for the lack of accomplished players. Although hundreds of thousands of the instruments are sold annually in many parts of the world, it is unlikely that many of these inspire the perseverance to attain any sort of proficiency on them.

The Jew's Harp Today

At the present time, there is still a small number of musicians who have developed a great degree of expertise in playing the Jew's harp. Foremost among these is the Yakut virtuoso Ivan Alekseyev. The Jew's harp is still a highly respected and widely played instrument among many peoples of Siberia, but especially among the Yakuts. Although he was fascinated by the Jew's harp from infancy, Alekseyev was not permitted to touch the instrument until he was twelve years old. Over a period of years, through unremitting effort, Alekseyev developed an extraordinary mastery of the Jew's harp. He has made several recordings on the "Melodiya" label and has organized an ensemble of Jew's harp players called "Altys," in which he performs as soloist, and that tours throughout the Soviet Union. He also lectures on the instrument at various schools and universities and is constantly active in the formation of youth clubs and ensembles of Jew's harp players. Alekseyev is now at work on a textbook of Jew's harp playing, to be published shortly in the USSR.[33]

In the Yakut ASSR as well, several individuals are working on ways of improving the Jew's harp. The Burtsevs, father and son, have been making instruments based upon engineering calculations and the younger Burtsev is now experimenting with the creation of new types of Jew's harps.[34]

In Austria, the Mayr brothers, Helmuth and Fritz, must be ranked among the leading Jew's harp players in the world. Aside from their recordings of Austrian and German folk music, in 1981 Fritz Mayr made the first recording of two of Albrechtsberger's Jew's harp concerti.

The Sicilian Jew's harp player Emanuele Calanduccio has been very successful in using the instrument for both folk music and popular music. He has made numerous recordings and is a great favorite of the Italian public. Another remarkably accomplished Sicilian Jew's harp player is Mario Ruspoli, who began studying the instrument at the age of fifteen. He has made two very noteworthy recordings, which include some of his own compositions for the Jew's harp, mostly in the popular music style.

Scotland, Ireland and England have produced several excellent Jew's harp players in the last fifty years. The late Angus Lawrie was renowned for his beautiful interpretations of Scottish bagpipe music on the Jew's harp. A young performer named Lindsay Porteous has recently been making a name for himself as a soloist on the Jew's harp with a folk group he helped to organize, and he has won several prizes for his playing at folk festivals in Scotland. Thomas M. Manus of County Fermanagh in Ireland deserves to be mentioned for his very expert playing;

he is one of the best representatives of the old tradition of Irish Jew's harp performance. John Wright, originally from Leicester, England, is a Jew's harp player of international stature. He has made at least nine recordings, some of which include a great deal of superb solo Jew's harp playing (Mr. Wright plays other instruments as well), and he has also distinguished himself as an outstanding scholar of the Jew's harp.

In the United States, Sonny Terry should be remembered not only for his wonderful vocal and harmonica performances, but for his lively and uninhibited Jew's harp playing as well. Mike Seeger has achieved a notable degree of proficiency on many folk instruments, including the Jew's harp, for which he has recorded a commercially released instruction cassette. Larry Hanks, Brian Minhura, and Tom Bilyeu are three more very talented American Jew's harp players.

Despite the absence of Jew's harp virtuosi of the calibre of Koch or Eulenstein, there has been a certain amount of music composed specifically for the instrument in the twentieth century. Perhaps the only piece that will be familiar to readers of this book is Charles Ives's *Washington's Birthday,* composed in 1909 and rescored in 1913. Ives himself stated that "from half a dozen to a hundred Jew's harps are necessary" for the parts of *Washington's Birthday* which call for that instrument.[35] To date, however, there has been no performance using more than two Jew's harp players. Frederick Crane has made a detailed study of the problems involved in Ives's composition and has also compiled a discography of the piece.[36]

In 1980, the *Concert Improvisations for Jew's Harp and Orchestra* by the Yakut composer N. Berestov was given its premiere in the Soviet Union, with Ivan Alekseyev as soloist. The work has enjoyed great success and is evidence of the widespread renaissance which the Jew's harp is undergoing in the Yakut ASSR, a renaissance due in large part to the great virtuosity and immense enthusiasm and energy of Alekseyev himself.[37]

Although most of his work has not been commercially recorded, the Canadian composer Eldon Rathburn has produced several compositions which include groups of Jew's harps, such as "The Rise and Fall of the Steam Railroad," "Junction," and "Ode to Eulenstein."

In 1984, thanks to the indefatigable efforts of Frederick Crane, the first International Jew's Harp Congress was organized and held in Iowa City, Iowa. Jew's harp players, professional and amateur, scholars, and composers from the United States, Canada, and Europe attended this event, which was marked by performances, recorded concerts, lectures, discussions, and an exhibit of Jew's harps from various cultures and periods. Such congresses—and more are planned for the future—ensure that those with an interest in and an affection for the Jew's harp are reinforced and supported in their individual endeavors. They also serve to help those who wish to play the instrument well improve their mastery of it. There is definitely a burgeoning attraction to the Jew's harp and its music in many places in the world at this time, and it is to be hoped that this attraction will ultimately lead to a reawakening of awareness as to the almost unlimited musical possibilities which lie concealed in this most unassuming of instruments.

Geo-Linguistic Survey of Terms for the Jew's Harp

This list includes all the terms entered in *The New Grove Dictionary of Musical Instruments* (1984) and those in Dournon-Taurelle and Wright's *Les guimbardes du Musée de l'Homme* (1978), as well as many not found in either work.

With regard to the puzzling English terms, cf. Frederick Crane's exhaustive discussion, "Jew's (Jaw's? Jeu? Jeugd? Gewgaw? Juice?) Harp" in *VIM* 1 (1982).

EUROPE

Albanian: vegël tringulluese
Basque: trompa, mosu-gitarra, muxu-gitarra, mosu-musika
Czech: brumle, drnkačka
Danish: mundharpe
Dutch: mondtrom
English: Jew's harp, Jew's trump, jawharp, jaw's harp, juice harp
Finnish: huuliharpu
Flemish: tromp
French: guimbarde; Switzerland: bombarde, rebaîrbe (North Jura), rbiba (South Jura), rbaîrbe (Freiberge)
German: Maultrommel, Mundharmonika (elegant nineteenth century term); Switzerland: Trümmi (Lucerne), Trimpi, Trimmi (Uri), Muultrummle (Bern), Tremolo (Bosco-Gurin)
Hungarian: doromb
Icelandic: munnharpa
Irish: trumpadh
Italian: scacciapensieri, ribeba; Sicilian: marranzanu, gnagnararrone; Switzerland: zanforgna, cinforgna, zinforgna
Norwegian: munnharpa, munnspill
Portugese: berimbau
Romanian: drîmba, drîmboaie, drîmb, drînd, drîndă, drîng
Romansch: timpan, suna da bucca, trumbla, tschinforgna, schanforgna
Sardinian: sa trunfa

Scottish Gaelic: tromp
Serbian: drombulja, drombulje, drimbolj
Spanish: birimbao, guimbarda
Swedish: mungiga
Welsh: ysturmant (North Wales), biwba (South Wales), biwbo, giwga, giwgan
Wendish: brumladeo

SOVIET UNION

Altay: temir-komus, komos, kobys-tyunyur
Bashkir: kubyz, kumyz; wooden lamellate type: agach-kumyz, agach-kubyz; metal bow-shaped type: timer-kumyz, temir-kubyz
Belorussian: drymba
Buryat: khur, khuur
Chukchi: vanni-yayar ("tooth-tambourine")
Chuvash: varam-tuma ("gnat"), palnay, jupas, varkhan
Estonian: parmupill ("bumble-bee instrument"), konnapill ("frog instrument"), suupill ("lip-instrument")
Even: kunkon
Evenk: wooden lamellate type: panar, purgip-kavun; metal bow-shaped type: kengipkevun, kongipkavun, pangipkavun
Kazakh: komyz, temir-komyz
Ket: pymel'
Khakass: temir-komys
Khantsi: tumra, tomra
Kirghiz: wooden lamellate type: komuz; metal bow-shaped type: temir-komuz
Koryak: vanni-yayay ("tooth-tambourine")
Latvian: vargas
Lithuanian: bandūrėlis, bandurka, šeivale
Mansi: tumran, suup-tumran
Mari: kovyzh, komyzh, kabas, umsha-kovyzh
Nanay: metal lamellate type: kunkha; metal bow-shaped type: myny
Negidal: konkikhi
Nenets: vyvko ("buzzer")
Nivkh: wooden or copper lamellate type: kanga; iron bow-shaped type: vych ranga
Oroch: kunkan
Orok: kunga
Russian: vargan
Sel'kup: pynyr ("hummer"), al' pynyr ("mouth hummer"); wooden lamellate type: pol' pynyr; metal bow-shaped type: kezyl pynyr

Tajik: chang-kobuz, temir-chang, changi zanona
Tatar: kubyz
Turkmen: kobyz
Tuvinian: wooden lamellate type: yash-khomus; bamboo or reed lamellate type: kuluzun-khomus; metal bow-shaped type: temir-khomus
Udegey: metal lamellate and metal bow-shaped types: kongkoy
Ukrainian: drymba, drumlya, doromba, organ, vargan, vigran
Ul'chi: panga
Uzbek: chang-kobuz, chang-kavuz, temir-chang
Yakut: khomus

ASIA

Afghanistan: chang-ko'uz (Mzbek people)
Burma: ata (Lahu people); rab ncas (Hmong people)
Cambodia: angkuoc
China: huang, koqin; k'api (Lutseu people): tivtiv (Ami subculture, Taiwan)
India: generally distributed terms: murchang, morchang, muchang, munchang, mursang; mursing (Tamil Nadu); gagana (Garo people, Assam); ghoraliyau (Rajasthan); tendor (Madhya Pradesh); ka-mien (Khasi people, Assam, and Meghalay)
Indonesia: genggong; rinding (Java), karinding (Baduj people, West Java): gogo (Gayo area, Sumatra); popo (Acheh region, Sumatra); druri bewe (southern Nias), duri (northern Nias); ego, genggo, robe (Flores); juring (Krui area, Sumatra); saga-saga (Pakpak Dairi region, northern Sumatra); karombi (Sa'dan Toraja area, South Sulawesi); oli (Minahasa, North Sulawesi); nago oa, keit besi, nago besi (Timor)
Iran: zamburak
Japan: mukkuri (Hokkaido Ainu), mukkuna (Sakhalin Ainu)
Laos: hun, toi
Malaysia: bungkau, turiding (Sabah); gurudeng (Iban people, Sarawak); junggotan (Bedayah people, South Sarawak); juring rangguin (Temiar people, West Malaysia): rangoyd (Lanoh tribe, West Malaysia); rangun (Juhai tribe, West Malaysia); jyrin (Sakai people, Malacca, Kelantan)
Mongolia: aman khuur, aman tobshuur; Dörböt tribe, western Mongolia: bamboo, horn, bone, or wooden lamellate type: khulsan khuur; iron bow-shaped type: temür khuur, tömör khuur
Nepal: bamboo lamellate type: binaiyo; kha-wang (metal bow-shaped type, Thakali people); machinga, changu (Sunuwar people); machunga (Rai people); kom-i (Limbu people); gon-kap (Tamang people)
Pakistan: chang, morchang
Philippines: kubing (southern Philippines); abafiw, alibaw, olat, onat

(Bontoc people, northern Philippines); afiw (northern Philippines); biqqung, guyud (Ifugao people); giwong, onat, ulibao, ulibaw (Kalinga people); ko-ding (Ibaloy people); kulibao (Negrito people); oribao (Isneg people)

Thailand: hoen-toong

Tibet: kha-rnga ("mouth-drum", cf. German *Maultrommel*)

Turkey: ağiz tamburasi

Vietnam: đàn môi; nggoec, tong (Mnong people); kong kle, kon hle, rhnui (Sedang people); göch (Rhade people); roding (Jorai people); toung (Koho, Sre, and Maa peoples); then (Bahnar people); guat (Roglai people); pang teu ing (Muong people)

OCEANIA

Cook Islands: pokakakaka; titapu (Rarotonga)

Guam: belembaupachet (Chamorro people)

Hawaii: ni 'au kani

Mangaia: tangi ko'e

Marquesas: hiva oa, tita'a kohe

New Britain Island: kaur (Gazelle Peninsula)

New Guinea: susap (Pidgin): begnankr (Buang people); bombom pumbune, tungge, songer (Biak and Tanah Merah, Irian Jaya)

New Zealand (Maori): kukau, rooria

Palau Islands: tumtum ra lild

Pukapuka: vivo

Samoa: utete (also used in Futuna, Tonga, and Uvea)

Solomon Islands: mabu (Nissan); tankuvani (Nasioi people)

tonga: mokena

AFRICA (local terms for imported European metal bow-shaped instruments)

Madagascar: lokanga vava

Nigeria: bambaro, bamboro, babore (Hausa people, also in Cameroon, Mali and Niger; Songhay people of Niger); zagada (another Hausa term)

South Africa: sekebeku, setjoli (Sotho people); isithokotholo (Zulu people)

Tanzania: koma (Shambala people)

Notes

1. Curt Sachs, *Geist und Werden der Musikinstrumente* (Berlin: Dietrich Reimer Verlag, 1929), 91, 92.

2. E. M. Hornbostel and Curt Sachs, "Systematik der Musikinstrumente," *Zeitschrift für Ethnologie*, fasc. 4–5 (1914): 553–90.

3. Frederick Crane, "The Jew's Harp as an Aerophone," *Galpin Society Journal* 21 (1969): 66–69.

4. Ole Kai Ledang, "On the Acoustics and the Systematic Classification of the Jew's Harp," *Yearbook of the International Folk Music Council* 6 (1972): 95–103.

5. Curt Sachs, "Die Maultrommel: eine typologische Vorstudie," *Zeitschrift für Ethnologie* 49 (1917): 184–202.

6. Geneviève Dournon-Taurelle and John Wright, *Les guimbardes du Musée de l'Homme* (Paris: Institut d'Ethnologie, 1978), 43.

7. R. Galayskaya, "Vargan u narodov Sovetskogo Soyuza," *Problemy muzykal'nogo fol'klora narodov SSSR: Stat'i i materialy* (Moscow: Izdatel'stvo "Muzyka," 1973), 328–50.

8. Ibid.

9. Dournon-Taurelle and Wright, 121.

10. Michael King, *Maori: A Photographic and Social History* (Auckland: Heinemann, 1983), 18.

11. J. F. Rock, "The Romance of ^{2}K'a-^{2}ma-^{1}gyu-^{3}mi-^{2}gkyi: A Na-khi Tribal Love Story," *Bulletin de l'Ecole Française d'Extrême-Orient* 39 (1939): 1–152.

12. Galayskaya, 343.

13. Gottfried Weber, "Die Aura akustisch und harmonisch betrachtet," *Cäcilia* 4 (1826): 49–62.

14. Charles Wheatstone, "On the Resonances, or Reciprocated Vibrations of Columns of Air," *Quarterly Journal of Science* (1828): 175–83.

15. Wilhelm Weber, "Etwas uber resonierende Luftsäulen und Lufträume von Wheatstone," *Schweigger's Jahrbuch der Chemie und Physik* 23 (1828): 321–33.

16. Emile Leipp, "La Guimbarde," *Bulletin du Groupe d'Acoustique Musicale*, 25 (1967).

17. Ledang, 97, 99.

18. Ibid., 101–2.

19. Cf. Dournon-Taurelle and Wright, 86–96.

20. Otto Chr. Dahl, *Malgache et Maanjan: une comparaison linguistique* (Oslo: Egede-Instituttet, 1951).

21. Sachs, 196.

22. Marin Mersenne, *Harmonie Universelle* (Paris, 1636), t. 3.

23. Gustav Otruba, "Die Maultrommeln und Ihre Erzeugung zu Molln: von der Zunft der Werkgenossenschaft," *Oberoesterreichische Heimatblätter* 40:1 (1986): 59–94.

24. Jean Paul Friedrich Richter, *Hesperus, or Forty-Five Dog-Post-Days: A Biography*, trans. Charles T. Brooks (Boston: Ticknor and Fields, 1865), 2: 88–95.

25. L. Schubart, ed., *Christian Friedrich Daniel Schubart's Ideen zu einer Ästhetik der Tonkunst* (Vienna, 1806).

26. Hofmann von Fallersleben, *Mein Leben: Aufzeichnungen und Errinerungen* (Hanover, 1868), bd. 1.

27. Rudolf Henning, "Die schlesischen Maultrommel-Kunstler," *VIM* 1 (1982): 10–22.

28. E. Deczey, *Hugo Wolf* (Leipzig, 1903).

29. Andrea Nixon, "Aman Khuur" in *The New Grove Dictionary of Musical Instruments* (London and New York: Macmillan, 1984), 1:52.

30. Brian L. Mihura, "The Jew's Harp in Colonial America," *VIM* 1 (1982): 62–66.

31. Otruba, Gustav, "Die Maultrommeln und ihre Erzeugung zu Molln: von der Zunft der Werkgenossenschaft," *Oberösterreichische Heimatblätter* 40, Heft 1 (1986), 94.

32. P. Dobrobaba, "Slovno svetlyy ruchey," *Sotsialisticheskaya Yakutiya* (11 June 1980), 3.

33. Ibid. and personal correspondence between Alekseyev and the author.

34. Ibid.

35. Charles Ives, *Memos* (New York: W. W. Norton, 1972).

36. Frederick Crane, "How Should the Jew's Harp Part of 'Washington's Birthday' be Played?" *VIM* 1 (1982): 49–57.

37. L. G. Il'ina, "O prelomlenii traditsii yakutskogo fol'klora v 'Kontsertnoy improvizatsii dlya khomusa i simfonicheskogo orkestra' N. Berestova," *Tvorchestvo kompozitorov Sibiri (Voprosy muzykal'nogo yazyka i stilya)*, vypusk 1 (Novosibirsk, 1983), 27–36.

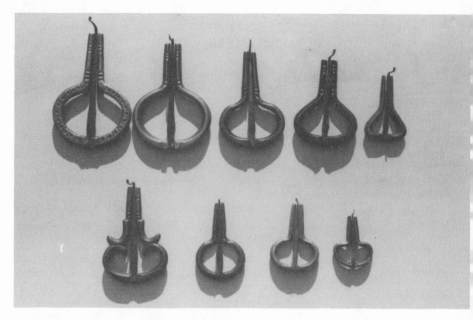

A group of nineteenth- and early twentieth-century Jew's harps from England and Austria. *(Author's collection.)*

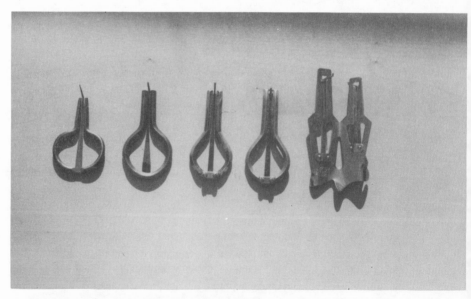

Modern Jew's harps made by *(left to right)* A. J. Wininger, Fred Whitlow, Tom Bilyeu (two examples), and the Austrian firm, Schwarz (double instrument). *(Author's collection.)*

The "Virtuoso Jawharp," the best Jew's harp currently available, completely handmade by members of the same family that has been manufacturing these instruments since 1620. (*Author's collection.*)

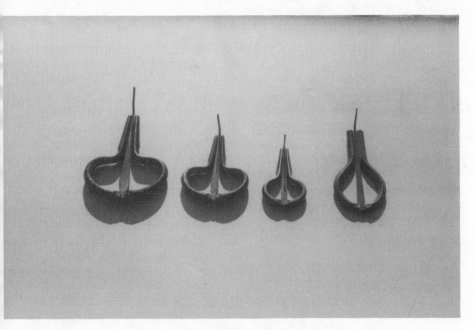

Four Jew's harps made by the Smiths of Rensselaer, New York. The three instruments on the *left* are early patterns; the fourth is the last pattern developed. (*Author's collection.*)

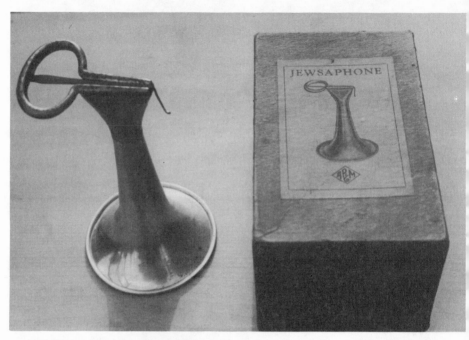

The "Jewsaphone," an amplified Jew's harp, manufactured in the United States during the 1930s. *(Author's collection.)*

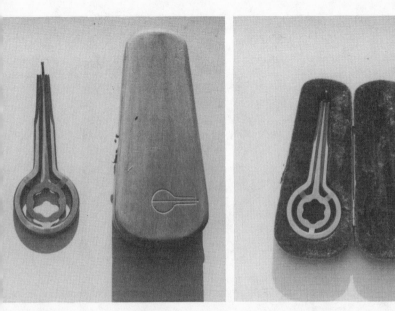

A Yakut Jew's harp, handmade by the master smith Burtsev. *(Author's collection.)*

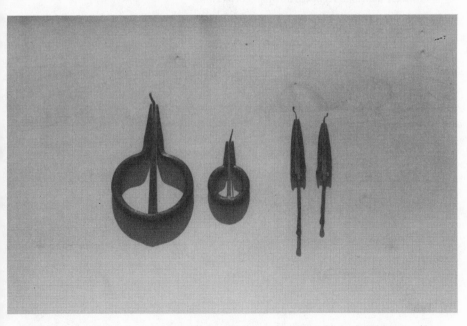

Hand-forged Jew's harps from Sicily *(the two on the left)* and Pakistan. *(Author's collection.)*

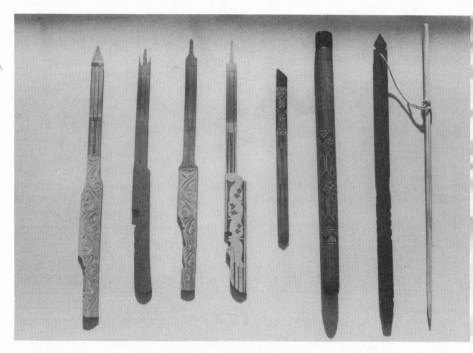

Lamellate bamboo Jew's harps from the Philippines, one with its case, and from Bali *(extreme right). (Author's collection.)*

The Jew's Harp
MME. ALFRED HEYMANN

THERE IS UNDOUBTEDLY no one born in the last century who does not remember amusing himself in his childhood by drawing sounds from a little musical instrument called the Jew's harp [*guimbarde*]. Contemporary youth, more difficult to please, has neglected this toy and is practically unaware even of its name. Its simplicity has gone out of fashion. The ease with which it was possible to acquire one from the toy merchants made it accessible to everyone, and everyone, in fact, played it as well as he could.

It seemed to us that its ancient origin, its worldwide use and, even more, the technical aspect, which certain scientists have elicited from the Jew's harp, merited recalling it in a few lines.

First of all, what is the Jew's harp?

The Reverend Father Marin Mersenne of the Order of Friars Minor, a French philosopher and mathematician of the seventeenth century, speaks of it in his *Harmonie Universelle*, which appeared for the first time in 1636. "Although this instrument is used by lackeys and people of the lower class, this does not mean that it is not worthy of consideration by better minds. It is reasonable to insert its picture here, so that those who have never seen it may thoroughly understand it: for there is no treatise from which it is possible to draw as much light as from the pictorial representation of things about which one speaks and about which one wishes to learn.

"The trump is grasped while its extremity is placed between the teeth in order to play it and make it sound.

"Now one may strike the tongue with the index finger in two ways, i.e., by lifting it or lowering it: but it is easier to strike it by raising it, which is why the extremity, C, is slightly curved, so that the finger is not injured.

"Many people play this instrument. When the tongue is made to vibrate, a buzzing is heard which imitates that of bees, wasps and flies."

From *La Revue Musicale*, no. 6, 1923.

XCVII *Spassa Pensiere*

A Jew's harp player by the Flemish engraver Arnauld van Westerhout. (From Filippo Bonanni's *Showcase of Musical Instruments,* 1722.)

Pieter Brueghel the Elder: "The Festival of Fools" *(detail).* 1559.

He adds that if one uses *"several Jew's harps* of various sizes, a curious harmony is produced."

We will see later that this idea was successfully taken up again.

The *Encyclopédie* tells us that it is a small instrument called *trompe, trompe de Béarn, trompe-laquais, rebute* and, most commonly, *guimbarde*. The term "trompe" is poorly adapted to the structure of the instrument: a trump or trumpet implies the idea of a large tube ending in a mouthpiece. A fantastic imagination invites us to take this word in the sense of "cheating time" [tromper le temps]: cheating the long hours spent by the goatherds in pasturing their animals or by the lackeys, who were obliged to wait for a long time in their porter's chairs until the caprice of their elegant mistresses determined that they should be taken home.

The *Encyclopédie* tells us further that the Jew's harp is composed of two pieces: first, the core, a steel tongue sealed at the end of the instrument and curved at its extremity so that the finger, serving as a plectrum, may pluck it; second, the body, formed from an oval of iron divided into two parallel branches, between which the tongue passes. The instrument is placed before the teeth and retained by the pressure of the lips. By moving the latter in various ways, closer and further away, capacities of air are established which vibrate in various ways. In proportion as one breathes, movement is produced in the instrument's tongue, which would give only one monotone sound if these vibrations were not modified by expert tactics of the lips and tongue. The player must arm himself with patience and practice for a long time before being able to obtain a satisfying result and draw profit from this rudimentary instrument, the simplest, perhaps, which exists. The Jew's harp player has scarcely any other means at his disposal than have certain whistlers who, nevertheless, by means of practice, execute complicated pieces using only throat and lips. Intensity of breath varies according to the force exerted by the action of the lungs. The use of the Jew's harp is therefore a bit tiring. Because of this, but especially due to coquettishness, women have spurned its use, leaving it entirely to young men.

It is told that a young soldier in the army of Frederick the Great was able, by means of two Jew's harps, to play artfully such sweet melodies that, charmed by his talent, the king exempted him from military service and added to this favor the gift of a considerable yearly income. Thanks to this royal caprice, the happy Jew's harp player, it is said, made a fortune by playing at court concerts.*

---

*The author is evidently referring to the most renowned Jew's harp player of the late eighteenth and early nineteenth century, Franz Paula Koch. Cf. A. Kahlert's biographical sketch of this virtuoso, translated elsewhere in this book.

The etymology of the word *guimbarde* remains unknown. Roquefort, in 1829, says that it stems from an imitation of the sound, "guin, guin, guin," which this instrument makes, but the explanation seems childish to us. What we do know with certainty is that the Jew's harp is of extremely ancient origin and comes from Asia. It was undoubtedly invented by the Chinese, like almost all percussion instruments. They call it *k'iu-k'in*.

It was the first *manufactured* instrument used by the Africans, because its moderate price made it accessible to their meager resources.[1] They used to form a group of about twenty and make their Jew's harps vibrate in unison in a very quick rhythm while their comrades, excited by their favorite amusement, would throw themselves into a wild dance.

The instrument's tongue, gentle to the finger which controls it, hums with a unique sound, in either a rapid or a slow rhythm, the tune breathed into it by the throat and tongue. A black musician in the orchestra so ably conducted by M. Wellmon, performing at the Champs-Élysées Theater, entertained us pleasantly by means of his Jew's harp with a perfect imitation of a locomotive on its route, from the faintest distant perception up to its noisy arrival.

The Jew's harp penetrated Europe and became ours in the fourteenth century. The oldest one known was found in 1360 among the ruins of Tannenberg Castle during excavations made at that period. It was discovered completely rusted, but it still sounded.

We find its trace all over the world, its name in all languages. There are few musical instruments as universal and as popular as this one.[2]

A novelist[3] and erudite professor relates the legend of Saint Jouvencel of Niklashausen. It is the story of a shepherd's life, illuminated by ecstasies and visions, in which our little Jew's harp plays a picturesque role. It was the inseparable companion of a young goose-boy, Hans Bohm, who was called to become an apostle of Christian ideas. Holding the rustic instrument between his childish lips and making the tongue vibrate with his finger, the young herdsman drew out sounds of a languishing sadness and imitated the plaintive sounds of the cricket. On the heights of the mountains, in the pure air, he made it resound with a clear sonority; his amazed geese clustered around him, stretching out their long necks in order to hear him, which flattered his vanity and moved him. Passers-by on the winding roads used to stop, charmed at hearing these mysterious sounds. But among his friends, his success was boundless, for on Sundays he also knew how to make his Jew's harp vibrate in a cadenced rhythm which carried them along in joyous round-dances. Later, when his illuminated spirit became that of a mystic, he would interpret the sacred hymns heard in church—until the day when, hallucinated by an apparition of the Virgin, he broke his instrument and cast it far from him as a profane object. In this tale, the words, Jew's harp, reappear on almost every page: this little instrument, then, affirms its use in Europe around 1366, the time assigned to the legend by its narrator.

The sixteenth century presents us with the surprise of seeing a graphic representation of the Jew's harp by the elder Breughel. In one of his humorous and realistic prints, dated 1557, *The Peddler Pillaged by Monkeys*, the latter are enjoying ransacking the packs of the merchant, who is sleeping under a tree. They are scattering his merchandise completely: stockings, gloves, bags, and Jew's harps are falling out of a basket which they have overturned. Still better, Breughel, in his *Madmen's Festival*, represents one of them making his Jew's harp hum to divert himself and especially to deafen his neighbors. The poor madman shows us very clearly how the instrument must be held in order to play it. In another Brueghel work, *The Wandering Peddler* tries to have us buy his flutes and trumps—the best there are, he says.

There is a seventeenth-century painting (in Gallery Six of the Amsterdam Rijksmuseum) by another Flemish artist, van de Venne, which represents the five senses in the form of five women, each with a different attribute corresponding to one of the senses; in a corner of the canvas, the painter has carelessly thrown five other symbolic objects: sight is represented by a magnifying glass, smell, by a pipe, taste, by some cherries, touch, by a scorpion, and hearing, by a Jew's harp.

Still another Fleming, the engraver Arnauld Van Westerhout, who was born at Anvers in 1666 and died in 1725 in Rome, where he had lived for many years, presents us with an Italian shepherd playing the Jew's harp. This attractive print was part of the curious work on musical instruments written by the Reverend Father Filippo Bonanni of the Society of Jesus, a work which was reprinted in 1722.

Finally, in 1809, the British painter, Sir David Wilkie, who, as a youth in Scotland, his native country, enjoyed going to fairs and markets and drawing all the popular types whom he met, painted for Sir Annesley, Earl of Inglessey, a picture on wood representing a peasant who is amusing his children by playing the Jew's harp for them. The little girl and the baby seem to be deriving immense pleasure from this and are attentively following their father, no doubt to imitate him themselves afterward.

It should be noted that the form of the Jew's harp has remained the same since its origin; the oval has certainly been modified in size, but the modification has been very slight. The instrument is not made in France; the great centers of manufacture are found primarily in Germany, the Tyrol, and England. This perhaps explains why certain English and

German scientists have especially occupied themselves with the Jew's harp.

Around 1812, Scheibler, Eulenstein, Kunert, Koch, and Deichmuller achieved extraordinary effects with it—to the point of performing and being acclaimed in concerts. These artists, in order to play complicated passages and change into different keys, used several Jew's harps without interrupting the course of the musical phrase. It is here, too, that we see the insignificant Jew's harp, modest instrument and relaxation of youth, become a scientific and utilitarian object in the hands of scholars.

Heinrich Scheibler made a complete instrument out of the Jew's harp and wrote a treatise on it, an actual method for Jew's harp. This instrument, he says, is of excellent help in rendering the musical ear more perfect. Singers, violinists, and all those who are obliged to produce *precise* sounds should make use of it.

In order to make known the construction of this instrument (which Scheibler calls *Aura*) and its method of producing pleasant music, we give here an abridged translation of the article, omitting the technical parts. We have included the explanatory illustrations of the instrument and a few examples of the melodies which may be interpreted by the Aura [these, in fact, are not included in the original article—TRANS.].

The Aura

The wish and hope that I might render a service to music lovers has caused me to write this study, whose aim is to make the Jew's harp known as a true musical instrument and to indicate its manner of use. Two artists learned to play this folk instrument and did so to such perfection that the most demanding ear would have been ravished by the gentle and melodious sounds which it heard. For a long time, in Piemonte, Ireland, and England, people have played two Jew's harps in alternation, but many amateurs have been discouraged by the extraordinarily mediocre capabilities of this instrument when used alone, as certain sounds may not be produced. In fact, without a special arrangement of instruments, it is impossible to hold several Jew's harps in the hand at once, and without several Jew's harps, it is impossible to obtain from them either the beautiful sonorities which they are able to yield or complete phrases. A group of five Jew's harps for each hand forms a perfect arrangement. It is necessary first to choose with extreme care those Jew's harps most apt to function well, having rigid tongues, without flaws, and in accord with each other. This extremely important choice demands great patience and an expert ear. The purity of sound produced by the tongue is recognized by its resounding without any alteration. In return for a small sum, the manufacturer of Jew's harps will agree to this long and minute examination, knowing well that your satisfaction will be the best advertisement for him and that this selection is indispensable to the perfection of the instrument. The chromatic scale is achieved by placing small *balls of wax* more or less at the furthest extremity of the tongue; these are, according to the requirements, of different weight. These details are very important for the success of the Aura. Once the choice is made, it is necessary to flatten the part of the bow to which the tongue is attached—not with a file, but by rubbing it on a soft round stone, so that no defects may occur in the metal. This is required in order that the Jew's harps may be firmly fastened between two small round plates prepared to sustain them. These plates must be cut with five notches for the placement of the five Jew's harps; they must be lined with glove leather, then put together by means of a screw, which holds the Jew's harps firmly between the two plates. The screw ends in a small handle, which is held between the thumb and the index finger; the tongue is struck with the fourth finger. The Jew's harp is placed gently against the teeth; it is surrounded by the lips and the notes are breathed by means of a slight exhalation, moving the tongue at the same time, as in whistling. A few attempts will rapidly demonstrate the best method of producing attractive notes.

Every Jew's harp possesses, in addition to its fundamental tone, the third, fifth, seventh, octave, ninth, and tenth, as well as the deep note of the twelfth. It is not possible to obtain any melody with one single Jew's harp; at least two, separated by a fourth or a fifth, are necessary for that. I mark red *lines* on the tongues of the right-hand instruments and *dots* on those of the left hand. In the pieces of music which I append here, I have indicated the notes which are possible for Jew's harps. I think that they will be easily recognized.[4]

Sounds which must not be prolonged are obtained by breathing out and in: the first note is inhaled, the second, exhaled, as, for example, the first four notes of the third part of Écossaise no. 1. *Staccato* is produced by squeezing the tongue of the instrument with the lips between each two notes or by placing the instrument against the lips instead of the teeth. The sounds may be more or less accented. In the dark, this produces a magical harmony. These instruments are especially suited to slow, expressive music.

Long use of the same Jew's harp is very beneficial to its sonority. Those which I have been using for six years are the best I possess. A little box, three inches long by two wide and two high, is sufficient to contain the whole instrument, once taken apart! Is this not the most portable instrument possible?

The organ builder of this place, Mr. Kamper, maintains a complete assortment of Jew's harps at a very reasonable price, in lots of six or ten, similar to the instruments described above.[5]

In 1828, the celebrated physicist, Wheatstone, took up this subject and wrote an article on "resonance" in the *Quarterly Journal of Science, Literature and Art*. It will be recalled that as a professor at King's College, he published his research on acoustics, as well as the discovery of curious experiments made by him with sound and the resonance of columns of air. In this article, he speaks at length about the usefulness of the Jew's harp from the standpoint of vibrations produced by the instrument's tongue. He explains the values and manner of producing gradations of sounds, utilizing Heinrich Scheibler's invention, and tells us that Eulenstein, profiting from the resources offered to him by the assembly of sixteen Jew's harps, is able to play melodies in all keys and produce effects which are truly original and of extreme beauty. He adds that those who have only heard the gross buzzing of this instrument in the hands of the inexperienced can have no idea of the melodious sounds which it is able to render in those of artists who have studied its use.

Heinrich Scheibler came to Paris in 1836 and, at that time, made known the acoustic experiments which he had pursued untiringly for twenty-five years. These experiments, like those of Professor Wheatstone, were for the purpose of determining with absolute precision, by means of the Jew's harp, the number of vibrations in the production of a musical sound, in order to deduce an infallible means for the tuning of musical instruments. It was in this way that, having sought a method for arriving at this precision by an arrangement of Jew's harps, he was successful in finding a perfect tuning for the organ; he communicated this method to the great Cavaillé-Coll, builder of our great organs, who appreciated it and was inspired thereby. Scheibler also profited by his stay in Paris to make known his new instrument, the Aura.[6] All of a sudden, the little Jew's harp, the shepherd's companion, the joy of children, was recognized by scientists for its "musical utility."

Count Ilya Tolstoy, son of the Russian novelist, in his recollections of family life with his father, also speaks to us of the Jew's harp. He relates his journey to Samara, where Tolstoy went every year to take a cure of fermented mare's milk. This *kumiss* had become a fashionable medicine under the name *kefir* and was prepared by Bashkir women; in this connection, the count describes the customs of his people. He speaks of their strength and he praises their skill in taming wild horses, as well as their talents in apiculture. Was it to attract these precious honeybees by imitating their buzzing, to which the Reverend Father Mersenne himself had compared the vibrations of this little musical instrument, that the Bashkirs used the Jew's harp, which they called *vargan?*

One of the Bashkirs played the Jew's harp very well: it is an original art. The musician lies on his back and begins to produce small, very tenuous metallic sounds: as the instrument is very small, one barely notices it and one would imagine that the music issues from the throat of the musician; one listens and asks oneself where these tender, harmonious, and unexpected sounds could be coming from. There are very few people who know how to play the Jew's harp; this talent was in a state of decadence at the time of which I am speaking (1873).[7]

If a serious philosopher such as Father Mersenne, a friend of Descartes, was preoccupied with it; if, at the beginning of the nineteenth century, the Jew's harp was elevated to the rank of a virtuoso instrument and taken seriously by scientists such as the illustrious physicist Wheatstone, the forerunner of the telephone, it nevertheless fell again afterwards modestly among us to the humble role of a popular toy. It was at this point, in 1859, that Lamartine, in his preface to *Mireille*, wanting to express how the poetry of Mistral enlarged and embellished all things, even the lowest, said: "A great epic is born. . . . A poet who makes a classical language out of a vulgar *patois*, a language of images and harmony which ravishes the imagination and the ear; a poet who plays the symphonies of Mozart and Beethoven on the Jew's harp of his village." Treated so disdainfully by the Romantic poet, the Jew's harp received its death knell from him and retired to the shadows, submitting to the common fate of birth, growth and disappearance . . .

The Jew's harp is still made in our time and may be found in musical instrument shops; but it is very rare to discover those little boxes of special shape in metal or curiously worked boxwood in which the Jew's harp players kept their favorite pastime. The recollection which adorns everything old with such a touching interest has caused them to be collected by a few individuals and by certain museums, such as the British Museum, the theatrical museum of La Scala di Milano, and others. They are unusual in that they reproduce the form of their contents; that is, like Egyptian coffins whose hollow interior faithfully follows the contours of the mummy which they enclose, these attractive miniature coffins also have the exact stamp of the simple and naive Jew's harp.

Who will make the little Jew's harps sing again? Who will know how to discover in their union the means of drawing charming melodies from them? Will some "curious person" attempt to resurrect this childish and naive but congenial art by means of his own naïveté? Who knows? Perhaps we have piqued the curiosity of this curious person!

Notes

1. In 1545 the English sold them for 10 shillings per gross (rates and customs).

2. The Dutch call it *mondtromp*; the Danes, *mundharp*; the Swedes, *mugiga*; the Irish, *trumpadh*; the Scots and the Flemings, *tromp*; the Walloons, *ystrymant*; the Russians, *vargan*; the Poles, *drumla*; the Czechs, *brumle*; the Serbo-Croats, *drombulja*; the Lusatians, *brumladeo*; the Slavonians, *brumda*; the Lithuanians, *drambras*; the Courlanders, *wargana*; the Estonians, *lotsapill*; the Hungarians, *doromb*;

the Finns, *huuliharpu*. In Spain its name is *verimbao;* in Portugal, *birimbao*. Italy, always harmonious, gives it the name *scacciapensiere*. In England, it is *Jew's harp*, but no one knows why, for the traditional harp of the Hebrews, with which David is represented calming the madness of Saul or dancing before the holy Ark, is a harp with nine oblique strings, without any analogy to the Jew's harp. Uncouth Germany vulgarly names it *Maultrommel,* i.e., "mouth-drum."

3. Benno Ruttenauer.

4. Scheibler thus anticipated the desire expressed by J.-J. Rousseau, who, in one of his letters on musical instruments, says that "if one were composing for the Jew's harp, it would be necessary to give the tunes a character special to the instrument."

5. Heinrich Scheibler, Crefeld, 1816. [In connection with Mme. Heymann's "abridged translation" of Scheibler's article, her work must really be called an adaptation, as she has added and interpolated at a good many points in the text, thereby even misrepresenting a few of Scheibler's statements. Cf. my complete and relatively literal translation of Scheibler's original article elsewhere in this volume—TRANS.]

6. Paris had already known Jew's harp concerts. Witness this document:

Concert on Friday, 3 March 1826

The Jew's harp has been, so to speak, an unknown instrument until today. Like the pipe, it constituted the relaxation of our shepherds; it is now taking its place in the salons and concerts. M. Eulenstein, newly arrived from Germany, astounds us with what he is able to draw from this instrument. By means of several Jew's harps, which he uses like spare parts, he plays the most difficult pieces with a ravishing harmony and charm. The sounds are gentle, prolonged and in perfect tune.

M. Eulenstein will give a concert this Friday evening in the Pfeiffer salons, no. 18 rue Montmartre. Distinguished artists will be heard: the singers, Mme. Dorus, MM. Domange and Brughiere; the instrumentalists, Mlle. Neuhanss, MM. Tolbecque, Benazet, Kocken, etc. . . .

The price of the tickets is 5 francs. They may be found at the residence of M. Eulenstein, 12 rue Sainte-Anne; at Poccini's, 11 boulevard des Italiens; and at Farrenc's, 22 boulevard Poissonniere.

7. Tolstoi, "Souvenirs d'un de ses fils. Voyage à Samara," *Revue de Paris* (December 1913) 498.

The Jewsharp
DR. H. CARRINGTON BOLTON

THE COMMON ENGLISH name of this primitive musical instrument is misleading, for it is not a harp nor has it any associations with Hebrews, as its appellation seems to imply. That it has nothing to do with Jews as respects either its origin or its employment is easier to demonstrate than it is to determine the real significance of its name, or the occasion of its invention. Antiquarians and lexicographers have attempted to trace the history and etymology of this term, but their suggestions are for the most part mere guesses.

Samuel Pegge, an antiquary of the eighteenth century, derives jewsharp from "jaw's harp," which is regarded by later authorities as absurd; and Skeat in his useful "Etymological Dictionary" takes the singular view that this name was "given in derision, probably with reference to the harp of David." Dr. Littleton, adopting the vulgar error that the instrument is Jewish, inserted in his Latin Dictionary (1679), the phrase "Sistrum Judaicum," a mere translation, notwithstanding the fact that the term *Crembalum* had been used sixty years before by Praetorius in his "Organographia." After all, the simple proposition of another writer is not so improbable as it might seem; he suggests that, after a long interval of disuse and of forgotten name, the instrument was peddled through England and Scotland by a Jew, and the name jewsharp became naturally the popular one.

Another distinctive name current prior to the nineteenth century was "trump," or "jews' trump," prevalent especially in Scotland. The earliest mention of this musical instrument known to the writer has the latter form; in Sir Richard Holland's "Duke of Howlat," a Scottish poem satirizing King James, occurs a long list of musical instruments, from which we take a single line:

> The trump, and the talburn, the tympane but tray.
> (Line 760)

This poem dates from the middle of the fifteenth century. The word trump is almost identical with the French *trompe* applied to the jewsharp,

From *The Popular Science Monthly,* March 1906.

as well as to several other musical instruments, the trumpet, the horn and even the rattle. Another common name in French is *guimbarde;* in German the term is *Maultrommel,* and *Brummeisen;* in Italian it is known by the poetical expression, *Scaccia pensieri,* banisher of thought. The word trump prevailed in Scotland, as was natural, considering the intimacy with France, and the phrase jews' trump was used by English dramatists until the end of the seventeenth century. Henrie Chettle, in the poem "Kind Hearts' Dream," dated 1592, wrote: "There is another juggler that being well skilled in the Jews' Trump takes upon him to be dealer in musick." In the following century Thomas Randolph wrote:

> O, let me hear some silent song
> Tun'd by the Jews' trump of they tongue.
> (The Conceited Peddler)

About fifty years later Thomas Otway in his "Friendship in Fashion" represents one of the actors, 'Malagene,' pulling out a Jews' trump and playing a tune. (1685.) Some wiseacre, seeking the derivation of Jews' trump, makes the suggestion that it is a corruption of *jeu-de-trompe,* but the guess loses much force owing to the simple fact that this expression does not occur in French.

In "Hakluyt's Voyages"[1] the instrument is called simply Jewes-harpe." The early explorers found these toys very advantageous as articles for trading with the aborigines; the barter of "hatchets, knives and jews-harps" is mentioned by R. Duddeley, in 1595, and one year later Sir Walter Raleigh wrote of the same people: "Wee should send them Jewes-Harpes, for they would give for every one two Hennes."

These baubles were also acceptable to the natives of Guiana in South America; R. Harcourt names them in connection with beads and knives. This trade with the aborigines of the western continent has continued until modern times; Mr. Joseph D. McGuire refers to it in connection with his description of a pipe catlinite carved in form of a jewsharp.[2]

In Bailey's Dictionary, which dates from the eighteenth century, the term is jewstrump, and in Teesdale's "Glossary" still another synonym is used, "gew-gaw"; this last name is also used for a kind of flute in Scotland.

This humble instrument of music, treasured chiefly by semi-civilized races and by children of intellectual nations, is but rarely mentioned in print, as its mediocre qualities give to no prominence in musical circles, and toys are seldom subjects of discussion. Sir Thomas Brown states that a brass jewsharp richly gilded was found in an ancient Norwegian urn; this suggests great antiquity, a point which will be discussed later.

In the report of those horrible witch trials conducted in the reign of

James VI of Scotland, in 1591, the "grave and matron-like" Agnes Sampson and the poor servant Gellie Duncan play conspicuous and melancholy parts. After horrible tortures, Agnes confessed that Gellie, Dr. Fian and herself, with upwards of two hundred witches, used to assemble at midnight in a kirk, where they were joined by the devil himself, who incited them to murder the king. On these occasions the devil always liked to have a little music, and Gellie Duncan used to play a reel on a trump, or jewsharp, while all the witches danced. And at another time when a large number of witches marched in procession to hear the devil a-preaching, Gellie Duncan, the musician of the party, tripped on before, playing on her jewsharp and singing:

> Cummer, go ye before, cummer go ye;
> Gif ye will not go before, cummer, let me.

The Skene manuscript of Scottish melodies, written about the years 1615 to 1620, mentions the trump, and William Daunay commenting on this says the jewsharp was the only instrument of music formerly known to the inhabitants of St. Kilda; and as this isolated, rocky island had only twenty-seven families residing there in 1793, Daunay's statement seems credible.

These few notes and the references scattered through that rich treasury for antiquarians, the English "Notes and Queries," are evidently written by persons ignorant of the birthplace and great antiquity of the jewsharp; examination of the collection in the U.S. National Museum, however, shows that Asia can indubitably claim that distinction, for the primitive models preserved there prove that these musical instruments are widely known throughout the Orient. They are common in the Chinese empire, Thibet, Burmah, Siam, and Japan, as well as in the islands of Borneo, New Guinea, Sumatra, Samoa, Fiji, and the Philippines. The Chinese call the jewsharp *Keou Kin*, "mouth harp," and consider it very ancient, and with some reason, for it is found among the Ainos, the original inhabitants of Japan, of whom a few survive in the northern islands.

As constructed by orientals who have not been influenced by contact with Europeans and Americans, their jewsharps are made of narrow pieces of bamboo from five to nine inches in length, and split so as to form a longitudinal section in which the jaws and tongue are cut somewhat like a three-pronged fork. A portion of the bamboo, of full size, is sometimes left attached to the split section to serve as a handle, and this measures in addition five to seven inches in length.

Often the construction is peculiar in that the jaws of the instrument are made to vibrate instead of the tongue, in which cases the tongue occupies an inverse position. In jewsharps made by the Ainos the vibration of the tongue is effected by a bit of bamboo fiber fastened to a minute orifice at its base. These wooden jewsharps have little power, and the modern Chinese, imitating Europeans, make them of iron with a projecting handle, which is virtually a prolongation of the tongue beyond the point where it riveted to the jaws.

Several native tribes in the Philippines make jewsharps—the Moros, on northern Mindanao, the inhabitants of the Sooloo archipelago, and the Negritos. In Burmah and Thibet, where the common name is Murchang (or simply Chang), they are not made by the Thibetans themselves, but by the Lissus and by tribes in the southeastern districts, where nearly all women carry jewsharps in ornamental cases suspended from their girdles. Melodies are played on three having a different pitch.

For the opportunity of examining the collection in the National Museum and information concerning them I am indebted to Professor Otis T. Mason, acting curator in anthropology, and to Mr. E. H. Hawley, preparator in charge of musical instruments.

The Waschamba tribe in Africa made a childish toy used like a jewsharp, quite unique in construction. Near the end of a pith-bearing stem is cut a small orifice communicating with the central bore, and a thin section of the outer bark or rind of the stem is split so as to form the tongue; this is vibrated by greatly striking it with a strip of wood, at the same time that air is blown into the tube through the small orifice. The character of the sounds obtained is not given by the ethnologist who describes this primitive instrument.[3]

In occidental countries jewsharps are manufactured on a large scale; they were manufactured in Nuremberg as early as 1524. In Birmingham one dealer, who made thousands of gross in 1895, packed them in boxes labeled "Irish Harps," a better designation for trade.

Regarded as an instrument with musical capabilities, the jewsharp was studied by the distinguished English scientist Sir Chas. Wheatstone in 1828. He wrote as follows:

> The jewsharp consists of an elastic steel tongue riveted at one end to a frame of brass or iron (shaped like a horseshoe). The free extremity of the tongue is bent outwards to a right angle, so as to allow the finger easily to strike it when the instrument is placed to the mouth and firmly supported by the pressure of the parallel extremities of the frame against the teeth. The vibrations of the tongue itself correspond with a very low sound, but being placed before the cavity of the mouth, the form and dimensions of which are capable of various alterations by the motions of the tongue and lips, when the number of vibrations of the contained volume of air is any multiple of the original vibrations of the (steel) tongue, a sound is produced corresponding to the modification of the oral cavity.

After specifying the notes yielded by a given instrument, he continued:

> This scale of notes is too incomplete and too defective to allow even the most simple melodies to be played on a single jewsharp, but the deficiencies may be supplied by employing two or more of these instruments.

And he refers to a celebrated performer, Mr. Eulenstein, of whom more anon.

The mouth forms a resonant cavity or sounding box, analogous to the body of a guitar, or to the stretched parchment of a banjo, the pitch varying with the form and size of the cavity; every one has noticed that in pronouncing the vowels *a, e, i, o, u* in their natural order the cubical capacity of the mouth is gradually diminished.

A few persons have acquired such proficiency in playing the jewsharp as to gain recognition in history and literature. Koch, a private in the Prussian army under Frederick the Great, played with extraordinary skill, and of him the following story is told. One summer evening, sitting by an open window, the king overheard strains of music of unusual quality, and on making enquiry learned that they arose from a jewsharp played by a soldier doing sentinel duty in the garden. Thereupon Frederick commanded the musician to ascend to his suite of apartments and to play before him, but young Koch politely refused to do so without an order from his colonel. "But I am king," said Frederick. "I know it, your majesty, but I can not leave my post, or I shall be punished." Although very angry, the king respected the sentinel's candor and fidelity. On the following day Koch, by invitation of the king and an order from the colonel, played in Frederick's apartments and so delighted him that the king gave him a sum of money and an honorable discharge from the army. Koch then traveled through Germany, giving exhibitions of his skill and playing in concerts, whereby he accumulated a moderate fortune. The chief attraction of Koch's playing was his descriptive music, pieces similar to the "Turkish Patrol"; he used to depict a funeral procession marching along to the tolling of bells, the approach and passing of a chorus of mourners, and their singing of an old German popular dirge.

In the first decade of the century just closed Heinrich Scheibler, of Crefeld, invented an instrument which he called "Aura"; it consisted of ten jewsharps of different keys grouped in two series of five each and fastened to a disk, with the bows towards the center, so that the jaws diverged like rays. With this combination he performed in concerts before large audiences, producing surprising and beautiful effects.

But by far the most eminent performer on jewsharps was a man named Charles Eulenstein, born in Würtemberg about 1802. He spent many years studying the capabilities of the jewsharp, and being an accomplished musician, he found that the best effects could only be obtained with instruments of different pitch, and he had manufactured sixteen jewsharps, on four of which he was able to play at once by connecting them with silken cords so arranged that he could grasp four with his lips. He appeared in London in 1827–8 and had great success playing in concerts and producing effects greatly admired by amateurs. Eventually his teeth were injured and he had to have them repaired by a clever dentist, who coated them with some glutinous substance that aided him in supporting the iron instrument. He also performed in Scotland and on the Continent; he was still living in 1878 at Ulm.

Wheatstone wrote of this expert as follows:

> Mr. Eulenstein by using sixteen jewsharps was able to produce effects truly original and of extreme beauty. Those who have heard only the rude twanging to which the performance of this instrument in ordinary hands is confined can have no idea of the melodious sounds which in Mr. Eulenstein's hands it is capable of producing.

Notes

1. "Hakluyt's Voyages," 3: 576.
2. Report National Museum (1897) 488.
3. Bernhard Ankermann, "Die Africanischen Musik-Instrumenten," inaugural dissertation, Leipzig (Berlin, 1902), 47.

A Brief Introduction to the Art of Making Jew's Harps
MONSIEUR BAILLET

THE TOWN OF RIVA, whose former territory extended to both banks of the Sesia, has several iron-working factories where implements are made.

The most remarkable of these are undoubtedly those situated on the left bank of the torrent, in the kingdom of Italy, in which Jew's harps are made.

About thirty workers in Riva, divided among ten to twelve different workshops, are engaged in fashioning these little instruments, which the Italians call *arbebola*.

The various operations necessary in making a Jew's harp are performed successively by several men or children, each of whom always does the same thing; the operations are both few and very simple.

One worker heats the end of a milled iron rod, 8 to 10 millimeters thick (fig. 1). When it is sufficiently hot, he sharpens it to about 10 centimeters in length and immediately cuts it to 4 or 5 centimeters from the beginning of the point.

He replaces in the fire the thick end of the rod which he has just cut and sharpens it in the same way as its other end. This rod, then, is 2 decimeters in length; it is cut in the middle and the two halves are bent, one next to the other, as is seen in figure 2. Each of these halves will be the frame of a Jew's harp.

The thick end of one of these halves (fig. 3) is placed in the fire, sharpened and given the form illustrated in figure 4.

It is reheated and then the frame of the Jew's harp is formed on an appropriate anvil (fig. 5).

Finally, the frame is finished by bringing the two branches together, making them parallel and of equal length, and the notch is made in which the steel tongue, or main part, of the Jew's harp is to be placed (fig. 6).

From *Bulletin de la Société d'Encouragement pour l'Industrie Nationale* Paris, 1806.

Pl. XXIII.

Bulletin de la Société d'Encouragement N.º XXVIII.

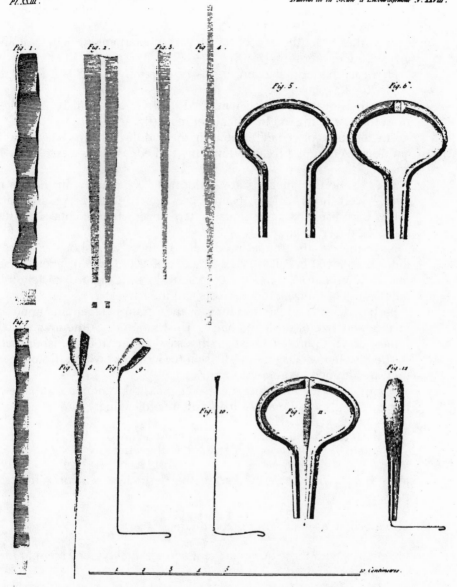

In order to make this tonuge, Bergamo steel, in milled rods 6 to 7 millimeters thick, is used (fig. 7).

A worker heats the end of the steel rod, sharpens it, flattens it and gives it the proper form (fig. 8).

He heats the tongue again, bends its extremity and cuts it at a right angle (fig. 9).

It is then heated red-hot, tempered in water and, finally, separated from the rest of the rod by a hammer blow (fig. 10).

The tongue is placed in the notch in the middle of the Jew's harp frame and it is fixed in by pressing down the two edges of the notch (figs. 11 and 12).

These various operations are performed very quickly. In the ten or twelve workshops of Riva, twenty packages of Jew's harps are made every day. Each package contains ten dozen instruments, i.e., two hundred dozen in all.

Nevertheless, the annual production of these workshops is scarcely more than 3,600 or 4,000 packages (i.e., 40,000 dozen or about a half million Jew's harps), since they are shut down for approximately four months out of the year due to frosts and the harvest.

Each package is sold in Riva for 5, 6, and 7 francs, depending upon the quality and size of the Jew's harps. This trade brings the town 24,000 francs, of which fifteen to sixteen thousand are in profits or labor costs.

The Riva Jew's harps are mostly sent to Genoa or Livorno, from where they are shipped to different countries.

I omitted to mention that the maker's mark is stamped on the Jew's harps. The principal makers' marks are the following:

1. the letter A and a sun; 2. an eagle and a sun; 3. a bunch of grapes; 4. a fish; 5. the letter A and a violin; 6. the letter G;

Jew's harps with these marks are the best: they sell for 7 francs a package;

7. a bell; 8. a small bell; 9. a mountain;

Jew's harps with these marks are of moderate quality: they are sold for 6 francs a package;

10. a flower; 11. the letters T and U; 12. a star;

Jew's harps with these marks sell for only 5 francs a package.

The Jew's Harp

KARL M. KLIER

THE TERM, *Maultrommel*, can be attested only late in German writing—first in Fischart's *Gargantua* of 1582,[1] although the instrument itself is traceable two hundred years earlier through a discovery in the ruins of the Tannenberg Castle, Hessen, which was destroyed in 1399.[2] The oldest graphic representation is a stone sculpture in the Exeter Cathedral.[3] This insignificant instrument was certainly in the hands of peasants and servants even earlier, but its origin is lost in the darkness of time.

In the year 1619, it was written regarding the little instrument:

> Crembalum, a Brummeisen which is made to sound by means of the human breath, just as with other wind instruments, and must be struck with the finger at the same time.[4]

Brummeisen alternates with *Dummeisen*, which goes back to the word *Trommel* [drum]. There is a quatrain which runs:

> . . . I kann singa, kann leiern
> Und's Brummeisn schlagn.[5]
> [I can sing, can play the hurdy-gurdy
> and strike the Jew's harp.]

Mund-Harmonika [mouth-harmonica] was first used for the Jew's harp by Jean Paul in 1792 in his diary sketches,[6] and subsequently only applied in connection with Jew's harp virtuosi and by them.

The expression, *Judenharfe*, occurs only in English (Jew's harp, Jew's trump) and is probably derived from "jaw's" or French *jeu* [play].[7]

The action is called *maultrommeln* [Jew's harping] (cf. the text of the musical example; a quatrain from Salzburg says of the Alpine herdsmen that they like to sit in the shade and "Maultrum'ln").[8] As a shortened form, *trommeln* is also used, for example at the beginning of a street rhyme from Berchtesgaden, where the boy announces to the women: ". . . muass Enk ebba was trummin oder an' Gasslreim sagn!" [. . . must

From *Volkstümliche Musikinstrumente in den Alpen*, Kassel, 1956.

play you something on the Jew's harp or tell you a street rhyme].[9] In older sources are found "strike" and "touch," as in J. C. Göring, 1654, "Our Myrtillo strikes his maul-trumpe"[10] and the unknown poet who wrote the Salzburg "Mosquito Net," 1694: "Where one sees the maul-trummel touched."[11] The expression, *Trumpe*, still shows the linguistic alternation between *Trompete* [trumpet] and *Trommel* [drum], although the instrument has nothing to do with either one.

The Jew's harp—in scientific classification, a plucked idiophone—is made in various forms out of bamboo or metal and is used over a wide area of the world.[12] The bow-shaped Jew's harp was so well known in the Alps about two generations ago that it was available in every little shop in the smallest towns and villages for a few pennies; in 1926 I acquired, from a merchant in Lienz, East Tyrol, the last forgotten instruments, which supposedly came from the Stubai. Knowledge of the playing and use of the instrument had already diminished considerably and had become a special hobby.

Only a few places of manufacture are known. In 1918 an ethnologist stated: "A few generations ago, Jew's harps were made by nail-smiths in Krain and on the Semmering; today, most of them come from Mehlis, Thuringen."[13] No other evidence is found for this, however. At the beginning of the nineteenth century, there were ten to twelve workshops in Riva, on Lake Garda, which manufactured over 200 dozen daily; they went mostly to Genoa and Livorno, as well as further overseas.[14] The oldest place of commercial manufacture, however, must be Molln in Upper Austria, not far from Steyr, where a guild of Jew's harp makers has existed since 1679; for the last hundred years it has surely been the only one of its kind in the world. In England and Germany during the nineteenth century, attempts were made to supplant Austrian hand craftsmanship by factory manufacture with iron casting frames; the attempts were unsuccessful.[15]

The history of the Jew's harp makers of Molln begins with the establishment of a system of craft regulations by count Lamberg, lord of the Steyr territory, in 1679. From its twenty-four articles, it is learned that iron and brass Jew's harps with the names "straw," "Pilsen-," "key-," and "Steyrmark-Trommel" existed. The articles of organization, as well as the guild accounts and masters' books, have been preserved in the Upper Austrian regional archives, and they give a vivid picture of the life of these settled, simple people.[16] The oldest financial office account indicates that in 1687 there were altogether twenty-three masters and ten journeymen. The craft was mostly inherited, like the house and land, within the family. Every master had his mark, which was fixed on a lead plate and kept in the guild center. He was obliged to stamp it on all of his products, so that fine work would remain protected. In the year 1818

there were thirty-three masters and fourteen journeymen, who produced, on an average, 700 to 800 dozen Jew's harps per day, or about two
and a half million annually! These went partly to markets in Vienna and
Pest, as well as Trieste, partly direct to Poland, Russia and Turkey, and to
wholesalers in Nürnberg, Frankfurt and Leipzig.[17] The craft flourished
in the nineteenth century to such an extent that a proverb stated: "the
scythe-makers beat Talers [dollars] out of iron, the Jew's harp makers,
Zwanziger [twenties—a far more valuable silver coin].[18] In 1935 there
were still ten masters, who produced about one and a half million
instruments per year in family businesses.

These large quantities were made exclusively in iron; brass was used
only for special shipments.[19] Individual amateurs had their instruments
made in silver: this was a source of pride for many.[20] Among the
Heiligenblut peasants it was said that there was a heavy penalty for
carrying a silver Jew's harp; the boys had once made people far too
foolish because of them, and the prohibition stemmed from that time.[21]

The manufacture in Molln is carried out completely by hand in one
large room of the house. The square wire is delivered from the factory in
large rolls—the smiths formerly had to forge the material in their own
small smithys—and is then cut or "divided" into the required lengths.
These are next stretched with hammers and the trademark applied. The
ends are then bent with two pair of pliers, measured, and next the wire
is turned at the edges and finally bent at the right angle: the process
proceeds more rapidly than the written description. The ends are filed
and hammered to a taper, whereupon the two pair of pliers grip the
piece and bend it into curves. The depression for the steel spring is now
made with a small press and the bow is finished. For the second part,
the tongue, small strips are cut from sheet-steel, the underside is beaten
flat, the upper side hammered and thickened. Filing follows, the in-
elastic pieces are removed, the end is bent upwards and the whole is
hardened. The completed spring is riveted or "beaten in" to the bow,
then the bow is "adjusted": if necessary, the ends of the bow are bent
into alignment with the spring by means of pliers. The finished Jew's
harps are now polished; they turn overnight, together with hardwood
shavings, in a drum. The shiny instruments are painted with bronze and
then mounted, four apiece, on wedge-shaped wooden blocks and
packed.[22] To protect the delicate spring, many players make small cases
which fit the contours of the instrument in the form of a shoe.

Clarity of tone in a Jew's harp is primarily dependent upon whether
the two cuts of the tongue stand completely parallel to the opposite
angles of the frame ends; clear instruments give the octave, ninth, and
tenth easily, and without any incidental sounds.

A Jew's harp with the fundamental tone in C has the following tones:

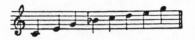

In order to play a melody, a second instrument of equal size must be added, tuned to an interval of a fourth or a fifth, so that a range of tones is built:

Tuning is accomplished by means of wax or sealing wax, small balls of which are attached to the end of the steel spring. The instrument is played by placing the frame against the slightly open rows of teeth, permitting the spring to move freely. The oral cavity is the resonator; by positioning the cheeks, lips, and tongue in various ways, other overtones are strengthened and made fully audible, so that melodies in the approximate range of one and a half octaves may be played.[23] The insignificant instrument is very important acoustically and harmonically, and is an invariable agent to true pitch. The rural Jew's harp player prefers slow pieces in broken harmonies, Steirer (see musical example), Ländler, waltzes, and song melodies.[24] An educated traveler reported in 1785 that "[a hunter] whispered an allemande for us on his Jew's harp."[25]

The simultaneous use of several instruments is already attested in the eighteenth century. Schultes, too, mentions a performance with two Jew's harps in his *Reise auf den Glockner* [Journey to the Glockner]. In Steiermark there were "natural musicians who played dances and songs without words with rare sonority and modulation on two or three Jew's harps."[26]

Individual men, through natural talent and continual practice, attained exceptional accomplishment and thus achieved renown and even wealth. Kaiser Maximilian I had a court jester named Guggeryllis who was an excellent Jew's harp player; Hans Burgkmair immortalized him in his series of woodcuts, "The Triumph of Kaiser Maximilian," of 1515. A group of virtuosi appeared especially in the second half of the eighteenth century, who brought fame to the insignificant instrument. Such a man was the Benedictine, Bruno Glatzel, born in Passau in 1721 and died in Traiskirchen, Lower Austria, in 1773. He played in the monastery of Melk before Kaiser Joseph II, on the occasion of the latter's tour of 1764, from written music, accompanied by a lute.[27] Albrechtsberger, who had heard Glatzel in Melk, later wrote several concerti for Jew's harp, mandora, and stringed instruments.[28]

Franz de Paula Koch, born in 1761 in Mittersill, Pinzgau (Austria), was a bookbinder's apprentice who fell into the hands of wandering Prussian recruiters and came to Breslau. He was discovered playing the Jew's harp during guard duty by an officer, played before the governor of Breslau, then at the royal court in Berlin. He was released from military duty and traveled all over Germany as a virtuoso on two Jew's harps, playing for Goethe, among others. He made an appearance in Prague in 1823 and died at the age of seventy in Breslau.[29] Another virtuoso from Pinzgau was Joseph Schnepfleiter, born in 1761 at Zell am See; from 1815 to 1831 he was steward at Seebenstein Castle in Lower Austria and "played the Jew's harp with rare proficiency."[30]

Heinrich Scheibler of Crefeld devised, so to speak, a theory of higher Jew's harp playing and recommended the simultaneous use of eight to ten instruments; for this he invented a special device in which three, four, or five Jew's harps could be clamped and a rapid change of key thus made possible. He called this instrument an "Aura".[31] His instructions were followed by Fr. Kunert, from Bohemia, who gave concerts with sixteen Jew's harps from 1821 to 1830 in all the German cities; he finally appeared in Vienna.[32] He was the teacher of Karl Eulenstein, who also used sixteen instruments and who went to London in 1827, where he enjoyed success for years.[33]

Its magical tone and simple sonority made the Jew's harp the preferred rural serenading instrument, which the boy played in front of the girl's window and which was, according to folk belief, irresistible. "A woman will do anything because of a Jew's harp," states an old saying which I heard in 1928 on the Blaa-Alm, near Ischl. A boy sings in a quatrain:

> Znachst han i Trumml zupft
> Zwischen die Zähnd,
> Und da is glei mei Diandl
> Zun Fensta herg'rennt.[34]
>
> [I first plucked my harp
> between my teeth
> and my girl ran
> to the window right away.]

This magical action of the Jew's harp's sound is also expressed in the legend of the instrument's origin. A sinner named Barbara had been condemned to death, but would be pardoned if she could invent something exceptional, completely new and useful. In her plight, Barbara made the first Jew's harp out of wood. Its monotonous but wonderful tones so enchanted the judges that they considered the condition fulfilled and gave her life and freedom. In lasting memory, St. Barbara was chosen as the patron of the Jew's harp maker's guild; her picture decorates the old guild sign in the parish guest house and it was also placed on the guild banner of 1691. This legend from Molln seems to be of recent origin: the picture of the saint was probably its starting point; it is a typical "inverse explanation."

An older stratum, on the other hand, is revealed in two Vorarlberg legends in which the Jew's harp plays a role in connection with "bogeys" and the "night people."[35]

The magic of the homeland, however, remains unchanged through time, as Julius von der Traun (Alexander Schindler) engagingly describes:[36]

The old nanny who looked after me and my brothers and sisters [ca. 1825] had a Jew's harp, but she played it very seldom, and then only when the nursery grew dark in the evening and we were especially quiet. Then I left my toy, leaned against the old glass cabinet and listened. I have never forgotten the sound. Our old nanny had formerly been a cowherd in the Steyermark Alps; my parents, who lived in that region at the time, had taken her into the house and then later to Vienna. As a boy, sitting in front of the Admonter mountains, I heard the distant sounds of cow-bells gently die away in a single tone amid the rocks reddened by the evening. I recognized the tone, for it sounded like the Jew's harp of my old deceased nanny, who used to tell us so gladly of the time when she was young and used to herd the cows in the Alps. I wanted to set a memorial in these lines to the old lady, her faithful soul and her Jew's harp: their like diminishes from day to day in the world and threatens soon to disappear completely. . . .

Notes

1. Kluge-Götze, *Etymolog. Wörterbuch* (1943).
2. Hefner-Alteneck u. Wolf, *Die Burg Tannenberg u. ihre Ausgrabungen* (Frankfurt a.M., 1850), Tafel 8.
3. *Illustr. London News*, 3. Juniheft 1933.
4. M. Präetorius, *Syntagma musicum* 2 (Wolfenbüttel, 1619), S. 5.
5. Enders-Moißl-Rotter, *Osterr. Liederbuch* 3, 27, 3.
6. G. Schünemann, Jean Pauls Gedanken zur Musik. *Ztschr. f. Musikw.* 16: 402.
7. *Encyclopedia Brittanica* (14. Aufl., 1929).
8. V. M. Süß, *Salzburgische Volkslieder* (1865), S. 70.
9. F. Kobell, *Schnadahüpfln u. Gschichtln* (München, o. J.), S. 155.
10. Grimm, *Deutsches Wörterbuch*, Bd. 6 (1885), Sp. 1810.
11. Leopold Schmidt, "Das Muckennetz. Alpenländ. Gesellschaftslyrik des 17. Jh." (*Sitzber. d. Akademie d. Wissensch.* Wien, 223. Bd., 4. Abh.). Wien, 1944, S. 72.
12. Curt Sachs, "Die Maultrommel. Eine typologische Vorstudie." *Ztschr. f. Ethnologie* 1917, 185–200.

Ferner: Paul de Wit, "Die Geschichte der Maultrommel." *Ztschr. f. Musikinstrumentenbau,* Jg. 46, Nr. 2. Karl Wehrhan, Die Trumbel, ein altes Musikwerkzeug. *Ztschr. f. Vkde* 43, 291.

13. Luschan, "Zusammenhänge und Kongruenz." *Mitt. d. Anthropolog. Gesellsch.* Wien, 48, S. 65.

14. *Erneuerte vaterländ. Blätter f. d. österr. Kaiserstaat* (Wien), 1817, 17. 9.

15. Vgl. Abb. S. 72 und Nordlind, *Musikinstrumentens Historia* (Stockholm, 1941), Tafel 19 u. 20 mit 3 Formen.

16. K. M. Klier, "250 Jahre Maultrommelmacherzunft zu Molln." *Tagespost* (Linz), 29. 9. 1929.

Dr. W. Breitschedl, "Die Zunftordnung der Maultrommelmacher." *Reichspost* (Wien), 1. 6. 1935. Ders., "Die Maultrommelmacher von Molln." *Der getreue Eckart* (Wien), 6, 1936, 198ff.

17. *Erneuerte vaterl. Bll.,* 7. 11. 1818. Für das ausgehende 19. Jh. vgl. Dr. H. Vitorelli, "Die Maultrommelerzeugung in u. uma Molln." *Volksblatt* (Linz), 1893, Nr. 136.

18. Anonym, "Zur Geschichte der Maultrommel." *Tagespost* (Linz), 8. 7. 1925.

19. Stücke im Technischen Museum, Wien.

20. Fressl, a. a. O.

21. J. A. Schultes, *Reise auf den Glockner* (Wien, 1804), 2, 152.

22. G. Goldbacher, "Bei den Maultrommelmachern." *Tagespost* (Linz), 31. 12. 1927 (ansprechende Schilderung der Erzeugung).

23. Gottfried Weber, "Die Aura, akustisch u. harmonisch betrachtet." *Cäcilia* 9, 1826, 49.

C. Wheatstone, "Erklärung der vermittels des Brummeisens (der Judenharfe) hervorgebrachten Töné." *Allgem. musikal. Ztg.* (Leipzig), 30, 1828 626–629 (nach: *Quaterly Journal of Science,* 1828). W. L. Schmidt, *Die Aura oder Mundharmonika (Brummeisen) als musikalisches Instrument dargestellt* (Quedlinburg, 1840). Mit Tafel u. Notenbeilage. (Not examined).

24. K. M. Klier, "Volkstüml. Querpfeifen u. die Maultrommel in den österr. Alpen." Beethoven-Zentenarfeier. Internat. Musikhistor. Kongreß (Wien, 1927), 373–377. Ders., "Bericht über phonogr. Aufnahmen österr. Volksmusik." *60. Mitt. der Phonogrammarchivs-Komm.* Wien, 1929.

25. Leopold Schmidt, "K. E. v. Moll u. seine Freunde." *Ztschr. f. Vkde* 47, 128.

26. Ferdinand Krauss, *Die eherne Mark I* (Graz, 1892), 34.

27. J. F. Keiblinger, *Geschichte des Benedictiner-Stiftes Melk* (Wien, 1851), 1, 1019.

28. Dr. Adolf Koczirz in: *Festschrift f. Hermann Kretzschmar* (Leipzig, 1918), 55–57.

29. A. Kahlert, "Franz Paula Koch, der Mundharmonikaspieler." *Neue Ztschr. f. Musik* 1835, 26. 6. f.

30. Adolf Schmiedl, *Wiens Umgebungen* (Wien, 1838), 2, 618.

31. Heinrich Scheibler, "Die Aura." *Allgem. musikal. Ztg.* 18, 1816, 505–512.

32. *Allgem. musikal. Ztg.* 23, 509 usw. bis 32, 110.

33. Karl Krebs, *Die Musikinstrumente im Wandel der Zeit.* Gartenlaube, 1910, 778.

34. Alfred Webinger, "Die Maultrommel." *Völk. Beobachter* (Wien), 24. 5. 1939. Ders., "Die Steyermärker-Trumml." *Roseggers Heimgarten* 7, 1883, 442, und 59, 493–496.

35. Seemann im *Handwörterbuch d. deutschen Aberglaubens,* Bd. 6, 4.

36. Julius v. d. Traun (Alexander Schindler), *Oberösterreich. Ein Skizzenbuch* (Leipzig, 1848), über Molln: 101–134. Vgl. auch: Justinus Kerner, *Das Bilderbuch aus meiner Knabenzeit* (Stuttgart, 1886), 291f.

Transcribed by the author in August 1926 on the Blaa-Alm, near Ischl.

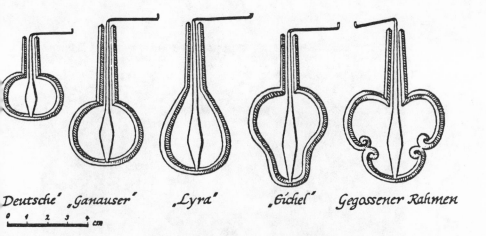

Deutsche'   „Ganauser'   „Lyra'   „Eichel'   Gegossener Rahmen

Jew's harp forms: *(from left to right)* German, Ganauser (=gander, as the form
of the frame resembles a bird's head), *Lyre* and *Acorn*—all from Molln. The
fifth instrument, with a cast frame, is from England. *(Klier's drawing.)*

Jew's harp player with one Jew's harp. One hand holds the frame, the other
plucks the tongue.

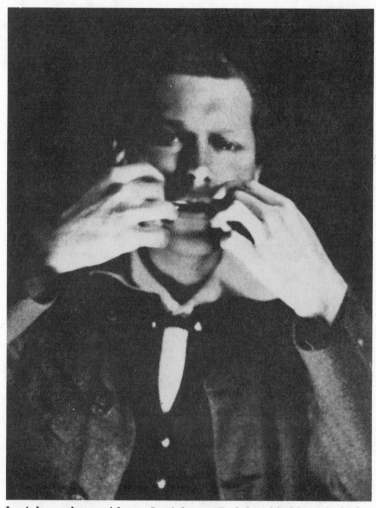

Jew's harp player with two Jew's harps. Each hand holds and plucks.

Court jester playing the Jew's harp. (*Detail* from the sheet, "The Fools," from the woodcut series, "The Triumph of the Emperor Maximilian," by Hans Burgkmair, ca. 1515.)

Carved Jew's harp case in shoe form from the Salzkammergut. (*Spiegl Collection, Ischi.*)

Jew's harp case in shoe form. In order to carry the delicate instrument and protect it from damage, young men cut cases in the form of shoes, with a hinged cover.

Table sign of the Jew's harp makers, hanging from the ceiling of the Schach-inger inn, Molln, with a picture of the patron saint, Barbara. *(Klier's photo, 1928.)*

Lead plate with marks of the masters of the Molln guild, ca. 1788. The plate (now in the guild records of the upper Austrian national archive) shows thirty-five masters' marks, mostly initials of names.

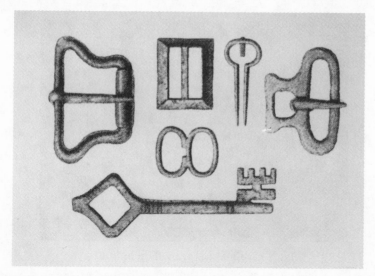

Excavated items from Tannenberg castle, Hessen, destroyed in 1399. Among these is a damaged Jew's harp, the oldest yet found in Europe.

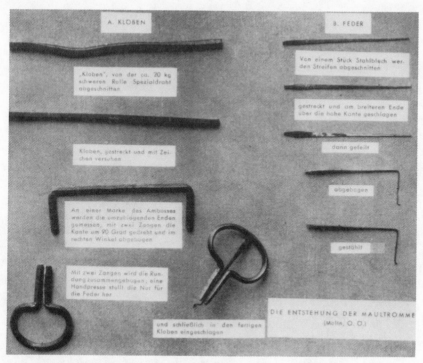

The manufacture of a Jew's harp, according to the procedure used in Molln. *Left*, shaping the frame; *right*, making the tongue.

Jew's harp makers' workshop in Molln.

Bending the frame with two pair of pliers.

Hammering out: the frame ends are hammered conically.

Pinching the frame: a small press makes a groove for the tongue.

Cutting the tongues.

Filing the tongues.

The manufacture is an old, inherited family employment, as this illustration shows: the man in front files the frames, the one behind him adjusts the frames before insertion of the tongue. *At the back:* preparation for shipping.

"In Molln there are twenty-nine workshops concerned with the manufacture of this instrument, as well as four in the neighboring village of Leonstein, which are also incorporated into the Molln Jew's harp makers' guild. The district of Traun thus has thirty-three masters, as well as fourteen journeymen, six smiths as assistants, and many women, children, and maid-servants who also work in this manufacture. An average of 700 to 800 dozen Jew's harps per day are made by these thirty-three masters with their journeymen and assistants. The instruments are first sold to the iron-mongers in Steyr and the cutlers in Steinbach, Grünburg, and Sirmighofen; from these places, they are shipped partly to markets in Vienna and Pesth, as well to Trieste, partly direct to Poland, Russia, and Turkey, to Nürnberg, Frankfurt, and Leipzig, where trade is accomplished." Such was the situation in 1818, when transport to the farthest lands could be made only by carriage and sailing ship. In this age of turbine steamers and jet aircraft, trade restraints due to regulations of all types are so great that the majority of the Jew's harp makers have been obliged to change their trade to that of wooden-ware manufacture.

Polishing mills in the Steyerling, near Molln.

Jew's harp player being recorded. Leopold Ainhirn of Altaussee plays on two Jew's harps in summer, 1928, during recording sessions for the Wiener Phonogramm-Archiv.

The Jew's Harp a Century Ago
ANTHONY CLYNE

JUST A HUNDRED years ago Eulenstein created a sensation in London by playing upon sixteen jew's harps. This expert performer played before George IV, and seems to have been a really fine musician. He had a very successful career in Germany before coming to London, and later in Scotland and at Bath. We must not imagine the instrument he played is beneath our notice. It is small and simple to make, but by no means simple to play with real musicianly skill. Unfortunately most of us derive our impressions of its performance from the raucous and unmelodious exercises of callow youths repeating vulgar and trashy tunes. Played thus, it produces excruciating cacophony, but so does any other instrument managed in a similar fashion.

A hundred years ago there was considerable interest in the instrument. Sir Charles Wheatstone, the founder of practical telegraphy, at that time published an elaborate essay on its technique in the *Quarterly Journal of Science*. Wheatstone was then an excessively shy young man of twenty-five, ostensibly engaged with his brother in the business in the Strand, inherited from their uncle, of a musical instrument maker. Wheatstone had gone there at fourteen, spending most of his time in researches in acoustics. His investigation of the jew's harp was but a small fraction of his vast study of sound and sound-producing apparatus.

Why the jew's harp should be so called remains an enigma. This was certainly the original form of its name, according to the high authority of the "Oxford English Dictionary," though no connection with Jews has been discovered. Some etymologists, uneasy at this obscurity, have endeavoured to trace the origin of the name to some relationship with "jaw," making out it was a "jaw's harp," others to some relationship with the French *jeu*, meaning "play." They have failed to establish any case. Of old it was commonly called a "jew's trump," a name that may still be heard in some localities.

The jew's harp has been known throughout Europe for many cen-

From *The Musical Times*, 1 June 1928.

turies. In France called *guim-barde* it used to be called *trompe*, a name still sometimes used, reminding one of its old designation in this country. In Italy it has various names, the most usual being *spassa-pansiero*. In Germany it was formerly called *Maultrommel*, or by some *Brummeisen*. It was in Germany that the interest in it of a century ago first arose, when all manner of novel and ingenious musical instruments were being experimented with. There the instrument was then rechristened "Mundharmonica."

The memoirs of Madame de Genlis first drew serious attention to its musical capabilities, by an account of the performances of Koch. He was a poor German soldier in the service of Frederick the Great. One night he was on sentry duty beneath the King's window at Potsdam. Apparently he thought to gratify the monarch's well-known love of music, for he began to play a pair of jew's harps in his most skilful style. Frederick awoke, listened, and was fully persuaded of being unaccountably serenaded by an orchestra. He looked out, to see only the private. He called to him, learnt the source of the music, and told him to enter and come to the chamber. Koch, suspecting a test of military discipline, respectfully refused, stating that he could not leave his post until relieved by the officer of the guard, and that if he did so the King would punish him in the morning for the dereliction of duty.

The next morning the soldier was presented to Frederick. He again charmed the King by his skill, and received his free discharge from the ranks and a present of fifty dollars. Koch made his fortune by travelling about the Continent, performing in public and private. He was accustomed to ask that all lights should be extinguished, in order that the illusion produced by his playing might be increased. A hundred years ago he was living in comfortable retirement at Vienna, at an age of something over eighty.

The peasants of the Tyrol had a practice, possibly they still have, of using two harps together, one tuned a fourth above the other. This greatly increases the range, and only by this means can really musical performances be accomplished. It is perhaps necessary to explain to the uninitiated that the harp is an instrument of percussion. A slender tongue of steel is fastened at one end to the base of a pear-shaped metal frame, the other end, with the termination bent at right-angles, loose between the arms of the frame. the frame is pressed firmly against the teeth and the steel tongue set vibrating by a sharp blow, producing a fundamental note and its harmonics. These harmonics may be isolated at will by altering the capacity of the mouth cavity and therefore its resonance. The lower harmonics are very difficult to obtain. The usual instruction to the player is to put the mouth as though pronouncing the different vowel sounds, though this is only an approximate description of what happens in the mouth of a really good performer. The niceties of the technique would require much space to elucidate.

By using two harps, with the difference of a fourth in the fundamental notes, an adequate scale is possible. What the scale is, every musician of course can immediately realise from what has been said. It was with two harps that Koch performed. The great Charles Eulenstein injured his teeth by playing so much, spending ten years practising many hours a day before he attained his mastery, and he had to relinquish playing almost entirely until a dentist found a way to prevent trouble with his teeth. He had an ingenious device. He used sixteen harps, tuning them by placing varying quantities of sealing-wax at the extremities of the tongues. He took each harp up as required, acquiring consummate dexterity in doing so swiftly. With sixteen possible fundamentals and their harmonics at his command, he could reproduce faithfully any melody he wished, and had an extraordinary talent for varying the timbre by some mysterious method of arranging his mouth.

The Aura
HEINRICH SCHEIBLER

THE WISH AND HOPE that I might render a pleasant service to the music-loving public causes me to make the Jew's harp, as a true *musical* instrument, better known and to give information about a device by means of which this may be accomplished, in that it permits quite a large range, as well as ease in handling.

A certain Herr K. [Koch—TRANS.] and, after him, Herr T. [Teichmüller—TRANS.], as far as I know, first played this otherwise disdained folk instrument in Germany with so much skill and taste that even the finest musical ear was most agreeably moved by its gentle, sweet tones, and the desire arose to become better acquainted with it. For a long time, however, it has been played in the same manner— especially in Piemonte—namely, with two Jew's harps. The two virtuosi mentioned shared their knowledge very little, or not at all, and were, perhaps, not sufficiently musicians to do so. Many amateurs also let themselves be put off by the extraordinary limitations of the instrument when they—as I—heard its range. Since Herr K. and Herr T., like the Piemontese, only played on two Jew's harps simultaneously (and without a special device it is not possible to alternate more of them quickly enough), they could not change over into other keys. Every music-lover knows, however, how few melodies there are which have no changeover whatever; and of these few, most are not suitable for the Jew's harp.

Another obstacle which stood in the way of making the instrument more popular was the inconvenient manner in which it had to be held in order for it to produce attractive tones. To learn this was far more difficult than the method of playing itself. The extremely beautiful, truly moving sound of the instrument caused me to seek a means of overcoming its imperfections. I provided Herr T. with six Jew's harps, together with a small device with which it was easy to manage them and accomplish the usual changeovers. Since then I have improved this device and, after many other attempts, I have added two more Jew's harps, so that by this arrangement the resonant bodies produce minor scales; the performance of many melodies has been facilitated by this doubling. I now use

From the *Allgemeine musikalische Zeitung*, no. 30, 24 July 1816.

ten of them and believe that the instrument is perfect enough to make something of it known.

Ordinary Jew's harps, as illustrated in actual size and form in figure 1, are the most practical for musical use. Among a number of these, the clearest and most uniform are selected. Merchants gladly permit one to look through their stock if one gives them a bit more for the instruments, as the average customer looks for a certain characteristic of the instrument, which also remains after they have been searched through, namely very rigid tongues. The clarity of the instrument is best known by its production of the octave, ninth, and tenth, and in deep ones, the twelfth, which must all be easily produced and without incidental sounds. Uniformity may be judged by whether very rigid tongues produce sounds that are too loud, and very lax tongues, sounds that are too soft. An excessive difference in the tongues produces a bad action.

By making small balls of sealing wax, which are softened and fixed to the tip of the tongue, the following notes are tuned; first according to a well-tempered piano, then according to the fourths and fifths of the instrument itself:

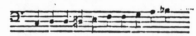

For the lower notes, the deepest Jew's harps are used.

Before or after tuning, the frames of the Jew's harps are ground down flat on a stone at the point where the tongue is attached; all must be of the same thickness, so that they may be screwed tightly into the instrument to be described next. (Filing easily harms the clarity of the instrument.) If the frames are not ground down flat enough, the Jew's harps do not fit tightly or often lose their good tone. It is only necessary to make certain during the grinding that the tongues are not displaced. The instrument—of which two are necessary to hold ten Jew's harps—is shown in figures 2a, 2b, and 2c in actual size. It may be made of horn and any pipe turner can produce it. One made of metal is more attractive and better because of its resilience. Screw a is passed through the wide opening of the cover b and screwed into the threads of cover c. The Jew's harps are placed on the cushions (as further described below) in order, between the covers, and screwed in tightly. The upper cover has five cuts and is very elastic, so that it holds each Jew's harp and renders small irregularities in them harmless. Both covers are lined with soft leather, not too thin, on the inside. The handle of the instrument is grasped with the thumb and index finger, and striking is done with a downward motion (never an upward one) of the fourth finger. The Jew's harps are placed lightly against the teeth, enclosed by the lips, and they produce tones by means of a gentle breathing, while the inner mouth and tongue are moved, as in whistling. Experience teaches the best ways of producing an attractive tone.

Aside from its fundamental tone, every Jew's harp has the corresponding third, fifth, seventh, octave, ninth, tenth, and, in the deeper instruments, twelfth; indifferently, the fifteenth and seventeenth. In order to find these, it is necessary first to exert oneself a great deal before one goes further.

With fewer than two Jew's harps, it is not possible to produce melodies. These both must be either a fourth or a fifth distant from each other. At a distance of a fourth, the higher instrument has the fundamental tone and at a distance of a fifth, the lower instrument has it. The notes obtained if the fundamental tone is C are—at a fourth distance:

1st Jew's harp
2nd Jew's harp

at a fifth distance:

2nd Jew's harp
1st Jew's harp

In pieces of music which remain mostly in the lower register, the fourth is necessary; in those which go higher, the fifth.

The ten selected Jew's harps which I use produce the following notes; in order to recognize them more easily when learning the instrument, I note them on the underside of the instrument—the left hand with dots and the right hand with red lines (fig. 3), or else write the fundamental tone on each Jew's harp:

Right hand

Left hand

In the musical selections at the end, I have noted which Jew's harps are supposed to produce given notes. By means of the above table, they will be easily found.

Although each individual Jew's harp produces only the harmonic triad of its octave (as do other sounding bodies without shortening), it is possible, with practice, to compensate for the second, fourth, and sixth in rapid passages by a pressure of the tongue against the palate (similar to that in the production of the sound *k*). It is always necessary, however, to end on a note which really lies within the triad (the seventh included) and, if possible, to begin on one of these as well. For example:

but not:

These examples are for a Jew's harp in G, and the hollow notes are those in continuity which are compensated for by the tongue pressure. The first and second parts of the Écossaise no. 1 give practice in these, while the other parts do the same in several similar modes of playing.

Notes which must not be slurred are best produced by breathing in and out, so that the first is breathed out, the second, in, the third, out, etc.: e.g., the first four notes of the third part of the Écossaise no. 1.

Staccato is produced by catching the swinging tongue of the instrument after every note, or by placing the Jew's harp only against the lips instead of against the teeth: e.g., in Écossaise no. 1, third part, 5th, 6th, 7th, and 8th notes. With good effect, two Jew's harps may be placed at the mouth simultaneously, *if they are separated from each other by a fifth*: e.g., the fourth part of Écossaise no. 1 and the first part of the Waltz.

For inexperienced players, it is useful, when they wish to play a piece that they have not practiced, to find on a piano the chords which the notes must produce, and then to write them down. An advantage of the instrument lies in the fact that one always hears, so to speak, the full accord of the Jew's harp and it is possible to strike one and the same note, according to one's desire. This gives (especially in darkness) the effect of a harmony, and it is simply, so to speak, the magical accompaniment of the instrument itself. If one plays a piece above G, or in G, or in C, for example, instead of E-flat major, it gives the same impression as though a singer who was singing this G in E-flat were accompanied by a C-major or G-major harmony. A trained ear easily detects this error.

One difficulty arises when it is necessary to change from one Jew's harp to another in the same hand, whereby an interruption occurs. In order to avoid this, I have placed the D of the left hand on the right hand as well for those melodies where the case occurs. In this way they are easily playable if played in G: e.g., the 4th, 5th, 10th, and 11th measures of *Nel cor piu non mi sento*. With twelve Jew's harps on each side, these difficulties do not arise, only this number makes the instrument very inconvenient and, because of the 192 notes which it comprises, so difficult to learn that few would devote themselves to it. It is also neither possible to find Jew's harps which permit these ranges, nor does the construction of the human mouth allow the lowest and highest of twelve such variously tuned Jew's harps to be made uniformly responsive. Melodies, then, which make such changes necessary are played according to the arrangement stated here: in G, with the D of the right hand used, as in the measures mentioned; or else the phrases are altered in the manner in which those in measures 4 to 5 and 10 to 11 in the first variation are altered.

Most melodies where *no minor occurs* may be played by the following six Jew's harps, and the first exercises can be easily managed with these:

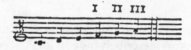

The instrument described above, with five Jew's harps in each hand, may be arranged for three in each hand according to figure 4.

Expressive music performed in slow tempo is especially suited for this instrument, particularly if the passages remain firmly in triads and do not require many continuous notes.

Rusting of the instrument is hindered, after it is polished, by painting those places touched by the breath with a varnish of the type used in the so-called gold plating of copper. The whole spring of the Jew's harp should not be varnished because it damages the tone.

If a Jew's harp which was good deteriorates, it is usually possible to fix it by bending the tongue up and down. The clarity of the instrument is primarily dependent upon whether the two cuts of the tongue stand completely parallel to the opposite angles of the frame ends. If these have lost their orientation, it is necessary to try and find it again. The frame seldom bends, and it is best to take another Jew's harp if bending the tongue does not help, as it is almost impossible to bend the frame without a special mechanical device.

A good Jew's harp becomes continually better with use and plays itself out—or, more accurately, *in*. For that reason, an attempt should be made to keep them in good condition. After a while, this care is rewarded by the instrument's greater perfection. I have some which I have been using for six years and they are by far the best that I possess.

If the instrument to which the Jew's harps are attached is made of metal, the whole apparatus fits into a small box, 3 Zoll [1 Zoll = 1 inch] long, 2 wide, and 2 high, making it the most portable instrument one can have.

In a short time, I hope to obtain Jew's harps of a more convenient form for the type of playing described here, and I do not doubt that due to this new form they will, at the same time, be better in tone.

If musicians or amateurs who know the instrument would care to communicate something to me of their compositions for it, they would do me a pleasant service.

Finally, I ask to be excused if I have occasionally gone against the rules of composition. I do not know them and my business permits as little time to learn them as it does to make the present introduction complete.

The new, more elegant name for the Jew's harp, *Aura,* I have chosen to use only in the title.

Crefeld					HEINRICH SCHEIBLER

Postscript. The organ builder of this place, Herr Kamper, supplies the assortment of Jew's harps described here in lots of ten or six, ready and properly finished, very cheaply, if one will send him a prepaid letter informing him of how his invoice will be paid.

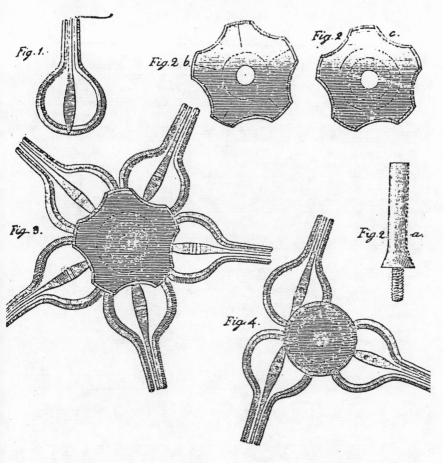

Fig. 1. A Jew's harp of that (actual) size and form which is best suited for musical use.

Fig. 2. *a.* screw, *b.* cover, *c.* base with screw thread. The cover *b* has five cuts in order to increase its resilience. Cover and base are lined with glove-leather. These three parts comprise the instrument of which two are necessary to accommodate ten Jew's harps.

Fig. 3. Five Jew's harps attached to the instrument; the view is of the underside of the right-hand instrument.

Fig. 4. Arrangement for three Jew's harps in each hand; view of the left-hand instrument.

2

N⁰ 5.
Écossaise
for the Aura

Both Jew's harps
are kept at the
mouth for these
eight measures

Thema.

Var. 1.

Var. 2.

Var. 3. Minore

Romanze
nach
Barwarzowky

Pieter Brueghel the Elder: "Every Peddler Praises His Own Wares" (From the series of Flemish proverbs 1568–69.)

The Aura or Mouth-Harmonica Presented as a Musical Instrument

DR. WILHELM LUDWIG SCHMIDT

The Jew's harp relates to instrumental music as does mini-
ature-painting to painting.

Foreword

The few pages offered here to the public are not the fruit of hasty
labors, but of many years of study, which the author was only able to
undertake in individual leisure hours alongside his real profession. He is
giving the public the results of his labors and experiments in order that
these preliminary studies of a special type may be used by the more
talented, that they may serve for a full recognition of the gentle instrument. The public stands before the author as a chorus of voices, opin-
ions, judgments, and decisions, and exercises an important influence on
the latter, as it does on the development of art. In many artistic endeavors, however, it must not be forgotten that man must be cultivated in
order to have correct taste, discernment, and judgment; otherwise he
may overlook or reject the unpretentious and gentle because it appears
insignificant, although it may be delightful and appealing, while the
predominant character of present-day music is tumultuous and agitating. The small instrument, though, fulfills by its fine delicacy the specific
purpose of music: to return us to that region of happiness and peace, of
gentle, deep perception which is our resting place. These pages do not
contain a theory without practical value, but a theory discovered
through practical labors; and they present this seemingly insignificant
instrument as a delicate musical instrument. Perhaps a favorable accept-
ance by the public of this instructional picture will also be influenced by
the excitement of something new and unusual! Correct artistic judgment
first results only from the spirit of artistic taste, but the friendly acknowl-
edgment of many, if not all, must encourage every endeavor; thus, more

Published at Quedlinburg and Leipzig, Gottfr. Basse, 1840.

perfect development is brought about desirably by both judgment and recognition.

April 1840

THE AUTHOR

Introductory Remarks

Why does music give man joy? Why does it cure illnesses, give new strength to the fatigued? Is it the feeling of order and rhythm which rule musical creation that causes these pleasures? Is it more simply the delight of the ear which experiences the fine sounds? Partly, of course! But the primary effects of the musical art are magnetic. Our self is composed of delicate fibers which are set into motion by the tones and vibrate differently, according to the nature of the individual. Music is, for the most part, of a spiritual quality; its roots are sunk in matter, but its fruits ripen in the world of spirit.

Musikalische Zeitung, June 1822

In our time, iron is beginning to play a role in the region of art. Pianos are built of iron and the metallic tone is praised; why should it not be possible to raise a disregarded instrument such as the Jew's harp from its lowly state to the higher standpoint of art by attempting to present the qualities and attractiveness of the little insignificant instrument correctly and simply? Even if the only motivation is a thirst for knowledge, it is easy to be convinced that no human learning, no human art is worthy of disdain, and to appreciate this attempt too. There can be no question here of wishing to give only a superficial description of the instrument in order to rescue it from oblivion. On the contrary, it is the author's intention to communicate the experience of a scientifically based study which, if it has not achieved perfection, at least gives cause for critical examination and information, whereby a certain degree of perfection may be later arrived at. It always remains true that the human voice is the most beautiful music for the human ear! Whoever wishes to discuss the little instrument must never lose sight of this. For in the wonderful natural sounds and in the double relation of voice to instrument and instrument to voice rests the inimitable magic of the Jew's harp, which I call mouth-harmonica because of the attractiveness of the name. But it may well be asked: What, actually, can a musician produce by manipulating this seemingly limited instrument, and what interest can a cultivated listener find in it? The answer is truly not easy. The tone of the small, modest instrument moves us like the sound of an Aeolian harp, more through the anticipatory wonder of the music generally than through the arrangement of some specific art form.

Music is of a purely spiritual nature and its kingdom is feeling! It acts upon our unconscious, upon our presentiments, and exerts its wonderful powers there. It happened to me in this way the first time I heard the sound of the Jew's harp. It was not a specific art form (as it later developed with me) which moved me; the strange sounds awakened deep presentiments in me due to the magnetic magic of the music itself. The primary effects of music are certainly magnetic; our self is composed of delicate fibers which are set into motion by the tones and vibrate differently, according to the nature of the individual. I found that these sounds were in harmony with my essence, and it was not very difficult for me to discover the technique of the instrument and to learn it thoroughly, as I had studied music from my youth. Unsatisfied with the manner in which I saw the instrument treated, I was delighted by the insights into the nature of the instrument which were communicated by Herr Heinrich Scheibler (owner of a silk factory in Crefeld, lower Rhein) in the *Allgemeine musikalische Zeitung,* no. 30, of 24 July 1816, and their correctness as verified by my own labors. If love and friendship are awake, remembrance never sleeps; may a friendly greeting, then, find a place here. During my travels through Germany, Switzerland, and Italy, I had the pleasure of being received in the friendliest fashion by the estimable Scheibler family in Crefield and of remaining for a while in their attractive home, so that I became acquainted with the manifold talent of my dear friend for higher mechanics,[1] and through his deft handling of the charming instrument, I came to the happy realization that its artistic treatment is not only possible, but actual! Whoever knows what countless attempts are involved in learning an instrument by one's own labors, an instrument which really can be learned only through self-study, will understand how to value the hints given in Scheibler's treatise. It is certain, too, that the delicacy, as well as the difficulty, connected with its learning will never make it a generally popular instrument; for the sound of the Jew's harp is, in relation to contemporary instrumental music, like a sigh which dies away unheard in the storm. Aside from individual observations, I do not know of anything comprehensive which has been written about the Jew's harp; otherwise I would not have been inclined to publish the results of many quiet evening hours. But as I believe that every sensitive person must feel the attraction of its magical tones, its echo sounds which blend into each other like the colors of the evening-darkened sky, I may perhaps hope, since some attention to the unusual is not easily refused, that with these pages I will give music-lovers a small gift for the embellishment of many sociable evening hours spent in a circle of love and friendship.[2]

II. Historical Outline

Among musicians, Schubart[3] was the first to consider the Jew's harp worthy of closer attention. Among our poets, however, Jean Paul[4] was the first to exalt it and raise the Jew's harp, otherwise banished to the lower classes, to the nobility of the harmonica.

The insignificance of the instrument, which is spoken of here, is not to be wondered at, as accurate information regarding its first appearance and the name of its inventor has been lost; but it appears that because of its sound, iron was put to use in even the earliest times. An important hint about the great age of the little instrument is given by the following remark which Maibomius (a learned man at the court of Christinian) makes in the third part (or section) of his little-known musical aphorisms: during the Eleusinian mysteries, the elders made use of the κιθαρισμός and the στοματίσμος. He adds that he does not know what the στοματίσμος was, but translates both expressions by hand-cymbal and mouth-cymbal. This remark is probably taken from the as yet unpublished manuscript in Uppsala, which includes individual chapters of Diodorus. The name *crembalum*, actually κρέμβαλον, may also be traced to ancient times. Ὁ κρεμβαλιαστής "he who plays the κρέμβαλον," once stood (Homeric Hymn no. 1) where κρεμβαλιαστύς now stands near φονή, 'tone, sound, voice'. Athenaeus 10, 14 describes this instrument in such a way that one may recognize the modern Jew's harp: τὸ κρέμβαλον[5] instrumentum erat, quod digitis agitatum, strepitum tantum edebat, quale illud puerorum aulicorum, quod parateur ex acie quod in ore artificiose retentum agitata digita ligula ipsius perstrepit, lingua sonorum discrimina figurante.

The little instrument, then, may perhaps have been known to the Greeks, but we find no further evidence of its existence. It is only many hundreds of years later, in 1442, that we find certain information that the Fuggers of Augsburg traded in so-called *Brummeisen* [Jew's harps] and sent great chests full of the small instruments to Russia. The use of steel springs in organ building may also indicate that the Jew's harp was known long before 1442 and that the utility of steel tongues for musical usage was recognized in this way. Thus, the organ builder Agricola is supposed to have used steel tongues to advantage in connection with the pipes of the Martinskirche organ, Groningen, in 1442 (Burney, *Present State of Music in Germany*). Kircher later mentions in his *Musurgia*, Rome 1650, that steel tongues improved the organ. Dr. Weber suggested a similar use in establishing pitches by using metal springs for compensation in the pipes.

III. The Names

I do not overlook the name. Resound, that I may understand you!

German: Maultrommel, Maulbrummel, Schnarre, Mundeisen, Judenharfe
Latin: Tympanum orarium, Crembalum
Greek: τὸ κρέμβαλον
French: Trompe à laquais, Trompe de fer ou de laiton, (Bombarde), Guimbarde, Gironde (perhaps from *giron*, "triangle")
Italian: Spassapensiere or Spassapensiero, Arbebola
English: Jew's Trump, Jew's Harp

AURA, MOUTH-HARMONICA

Nothing may be learned from the name, one may well think; but it seems to me that the name must denote the object correctly if it is to be appropriately called. The name is therefore in no way indifferent, but must describe the characteristic form or nature of the instrument. The German names, although the usual ones for the little instrument are not very attractive, have something descriptive about them: *Brummeisen* [humming, buzzing iron] or *Maultrommel* [mouth-drum]; for, badly used, it does give out a buzzing tone, one might even say a droning tone, like a drum. The names *Maulbrummel* and *Schnarre* are mere provincialisms, for a grumbling [Gebrummel] is certainly not pleasant to hear, and a particular Jew's harp which has a rattling [schnarrende] or clinking tone is not suitable for musical use. The term *Mundeisen* [mouth-iron], which Chladni suggested because of the instrument's melodious sound (see his contributions on practical acoustics, etc.), is entirely unsuitable and too affected, as there are many iron instruments played with the mouth, while the name *Judenharfe* [lit. Jew's harp] seems to be used mockingly. These four names, then, may be rejected as being unsuitable. The Latin term *tympanum orarium* does not appear to be completely incorrect, if one considers the striking and vibrations of the instrument's tongue. The name *crembalum* is not Latin, but comes from the Greek τὸ κρέμβαλον, and at least gives a hint (?) as to the age of the little instrument. Of the names given by the French to the instrument, *trompe à laquais* [lackey's trump] is certainly the most unsuitable; the others can at least be explained. That it is called *trompe de fer ou de laiton* is quite accurate, for the little instrument has, when properly handled, a fine trumpet-like tone and is made of either iron or brass. The names *bombarde, gironde,* and *guimbarde* may also be explained. In organ building, the bass drone is called *la bombarde,* the *bombardo,* and as a description of one characteristic, the name would not be totally wrong, since the fundamental tone always resonates when playing the instrument. *Gironde* perhaps comes from *giron,* a triangle, since the oldest instruments are triangularly shaped. The little instrument is called *guimbarde* in the *Bulletin de la Société d'encouragement pour l'industrie nationale*, cinquième année, Paris, 1806, p. 101; the writer must therefore have an adequate basis for this name. The Italians call the instrument *spassapensiere* or *spassapensiero* (perhaps "pastime"). In Italy, I only heard it called— very attractively—*arbebola*, although no one could explain the reason for this name to me. The English designation, *Jew's trump* or *Jew's harp*, is to be explained in the same way as the German term mentioned above, but contains nothing in the least characteristic.

I do not want to go against linguistic usage in this little work, particularly not against general understanding; for that reason, when I speak of single instruments, I will use the names *Brummeisen* or *Maultrommel* [translated here throughout as Jew's harp—TRANS.], but for the assembled instrument used for music, the most suitable denominations seem to me to be *Aura* or *Mouth-harmonica*. In its assembled form, the Jew's harp is most similar to the harmonica: it has the same swelling tones, the same resounding echo sounds, the same magical effect on the nervous system. The human mouth constructs the instrument by means of an iron rod, in the middle of which there is a vibrating tongue made of sheet-steel; the tones seem to come from deep within the human breast and to vanish into the gentle, unnoticeable breath of the listener. Is, then, the name Mouth-harmonica not characteristic and correct? Heinrich Scheibler called it *Aura* (i.e., gentle breeze), which suited the elegant and very fitting composition of individual Jew's harps, just as it, so to speak, described the gentle breath which makes it possible to lure forth the wonderful, delicate tones from the trembling tongue of the instrument. It therefore seems that the double designation Aura[7] or Mouth-harmonica embraces the characteristics of the little instrument, and for that reason I have chosen them too. Certainly, the Jew's harp in its simplicity is insufficient, but the composition of many of them into one instrument with the designation Aura or Mouth-harmonica made it possible to satisfy the artist's wishes.

IV. Material and Form

> Material is the visible, the spirit which dwells therein, the invisible; the particular material is the house of the particular spirit. Today, everyone makes war on form, yet it is only through the form that the soul is manifested!

Iron has always been used to make Jew's harps, even if brass and nobler metals were used later, and today the little instruments are still made of iron, as they were formerly. Iron is preferable to all other metals for musical use because it is easy to work with, because of its resonance—nothing resounds like steel—and because it is cheap. The musician may thus select the best sounding instruments from a great number—easily and without much expenditure. Brass instruments are considerably more expensive and by no means have the beautiful tone. Instruments made of silver are pleasant to handle, because of the softness of the metal; the same holds true for those made of gold, but to a higher degree. What makes the production in gold and silver difficult is the cost of the metals themselves and the consequent loss of a larger selection. Needless to say, when we speak of making the little instruments out of brass, copper, pinchbeck, silver, and gold—all of which are used for the instrument, these materials are used only for the form of the instrument, i.e., the rod which is bent into a more or less lyre-like shape around the tongue, but never for the tongue, which must always be made of steel. I have tried brass, copper, pinchbeck, silver, and gold, and have had the little instrument made under my own eyes and according to my directions; and I confess that I have spared neither labor nor cost, so that I possess some very excellent instruments.

The oldest form of this instrument that I have been able to discover is the triangle; it is possible that the triangle (the well-known instrument) occasioned the invention of the Jew's harp. The steel tongue is firmly fixed to the base of the triangle, in its middle. After it has cut through the middle of the actual triangle, the square rods, from which the triangle is made (and which I call bars), extend on both sides and surround it. The tongue, which lies horizontally, raises its point where the bars end, perpendicularly to a height of ½ to ¾ of an inch and is slightly curved at its extreme end, in order to facilitate striking. As this form had a poor sound and was also inconvenient to use, it was soon changed, for one finds few of this type now. The square rods, which are about ⅛" in thickness, were bent to have more roundness in the body, a lyre form, even if imitated in a careless manner, and thus the Jew's harps came about which are now best suited for musical use. The larger and smaller forms of these are illustrated in natural size on plate 1, nos. 3 and 4. Most people who play this instrument in an artistic manner use the larger form (plate 1, no. 3), whereas I, for my musical use, prefer the smaller (plate 2, no. 4), as does my dear friend Heinrich Scheibler. As the instruments are manufactured in brass, as well as in iron, I notice that the former are almost the same size as that of no. 3 on plate 1, although the majority which reach the market are of the size illustrated in nos. 1 and 2 of plate 2. A newer form, made especially by the skilled master locksmith Sigismund Ventner of Klein Schmalkalden, near Gotha, who also tunes and finishes them very well, is drawn in actual size on plate 2, nos. 3 and 4.

The smallest type of instrument which I have found is illustrated on plate 1, no. 5, and it is included only for the sake of completeness.

There are also instruments with two and three iron tongues inserted, but these are of no real musical use. I have succeeded in an effort to make the form of this instrument more attractive and to bring it closer to a lyre form, as plate 3 illustrates. The instruments pictured on this plate are made of silver and gold, and are certainly sufficient to the requirements made of them by art. No. 1 shows an instrument of which I possess three in gold and three in silver; it is drawn to actual size. The steel tongue lies completely free in a depression in the frame, only pressed down and held firmly by a steel lamella attached with two small steel screws. No. 2 shows the tongue and the thickness of the bars, as well as their form. No. 3 gives a view of an instrument made of silver with two tongues. It is evident that the tongues must have a different form in order to fit such an instrument, for they have a straight line on the side of the middle rod or bar and are broader only on the freer sides. Both tongues are held by three small screws, in the same manner as mentioned above. The instrument is for the right hand; for that reason, the lower tongue is shorter, because otherwise the tongues could not be struck either individually or together in order to set them in motion. No. 4 shows the position of the tongues, as well as the form and thickness of the bars. No. 5 indicates for the maker the position of the middle bar and one part of the frame. Everything else is clear from the view. This two-tongued instrument is very conveniently suited for musical use, although it requires a great deal of practice in handling. The three-tongued instrument is made in the same way, but is, as experience has taught me, very inconvenient. I will take the opportunity below to give views and descriptions of the formal composition of many small instruments into a practical musical whole. It seems fitting to me to close this section on material and form with an outline of the manufacture of this instrument, which certainly belongs here. This instrument is such an easy task for the iron-worker that it may seem laughable for me to explain it; for it is simple to construct the frame and bars of the instrument from square-hammered iron rods, for which ordinary iron is suited; its easy manufacture is also expressed in its cheapness. Needless to say, devices are necessary for the forms, because the small rod flakes easily, resulting in unevennesses which easily make the little instrument unusable. What is not so simple, however, is the hardening of the steel, so that the steel tongue is neither too soft nor too brittle, as well as the firm, straight, and even insertion and attachment of the tongue, upon which everything depends. I would refer here to the article mentioned above ("Notice sur l'art de fabriquer les guimbardes . . .) [translated elsewhere in this volume—TRANS.] and to the experience of those who are concerned with the production of steel springs, such as those used extensively in musical clocks, shawms, and physharmonicas.

V. Essence and Type of Music

With certain materials, it seems as though nature has set the tones directly in accord and, without theory and scales, has inspired them with the laws of eternal harmony. How it calls to the spirit—disdaining any interference by art—from the simple strings of the aeolian harp, and what wonderful sounds of harps and music of the spheres has it imparted to the raw iron of a Jew's harp. Here, breath and finger only help to make the spirit air, through tones which nature has imbued, and so the heart responds no less to the iron tongue of the dead metal than to the living, sensitive singer. Such instruments cannot be classified under any rubric; they stand alone and outside all connection with a sounding environment which dissolves them and would destroy their action and essence.

Iris, no. 10, March 1820

With the words of the motto of this section, the essence of the wonderful little instrument is most strikingly portrayed, and it requires only a simple analysis to make it generally comprehensible. The inimitable magic of the Jew's harp most assuredly lies in its wonderful natural sounds and in the double relation of the voice to the instrument and the instrument to the voice. One cannot say without theory and scales, for both find their application in the study of the instrument, but certainly the instrument appears to be imbued in a mysterious manner with eternal harmonies which call to the spirit or which are, I would prefer to say, soulful. We correctly sense that such music is of a purely spiritual nature, even if feeling is the realm of all music, for it acts on the unconsicous, on the presentiment in us, and exercises the wonderful power there. The gentle aids of breath and finger, which are employed simply to make spirit air, i.e., to manifest it, speak themselves for the delicate essence of the instrument; but even more, for its action, which is exerted on the bearers of the spiritual life, the nerves. In order to understand the essence of the little instrument, the musician must be initiated into the secret of this silent magic, for no mouth can speak, no teaching embrace or communicate the sound and song united in a whole with the gentle vibration transferred from one soul to another, leading the listener to a region where everything appears to stream with greater purity, clarity, and love. The Jew's harp, therefore, fulfills the essential condition of music, which can only be to return us to a region of gently soothing wistfulness, of happiness and peace, which is our real resting place. There is, perhaps, no other instrument on earth which finds its way to the spirit so quickly and surely as does this one. If the artistic power of an instrument thrills us with admiration, we must be in the mood for it; but natural sounds always move us when they reach our ear, and no matter how often we hear them, they are always new and enchanting for us, like the memories of youth which resound throughout our lives from a magical distance. If the natural sounds are excellently produced on the little instrument and deeply move the listener, then it is true that simplicity is part of the essence of this instrument; even simple melodies are well suited for this. It is also the melody, though, which reaches the heart and moves the feelings, and an instrument like the Jew's harp is most beautifully described if it is called a vocal one, for every true melody must be able to be sung. The understated tones, the aspiration, fine touches and blendings of the voice with the instrument form its delicacy and inimitable magic, as the expression of delicate sensations constitutes the subtle person. It is naturally a marvelous attribute that it is not necessary for the subject always to be a fine one where the instrument is used, in order for it still to have appeal. The Jew's harp exercises this power of attraction with simple melodies, chorales, marches, and free fantasies, when it sounds as pure as bells, as gentle and mild as flutes, as strong as the horn, and as penetrating as trombones and trumpets, but always amazingly correct and completely harmonic in the rise and fall of expression when the sounds are elevated from breath to breath and finally die away like distant echoes. Is it not possible to say that, just as understanding and feeling are united in every exalted musical pleasure, the true delicacy of the Jew's harp's natural tones, whose purity moves us by setting the tones of our perceptions into vibration in stimulating light and darkness, increases the magical poweer of the instrument in precisely this way? Whoever has had the opportunity, even once, to hear the little instrument played with greater or lesser perfection, will have felt the magical impression which it gives. In order to hear the Jew's harp clearly and pleasurably, particular attention is required, a straining of the nerves, so to speak, particularly those of the organs of hearing. For that reason, its action on the nerves is easy to explain. As a physician, I have become acquainted in many ways with the effects of music, with which I have occupied myself since my youth—alone and without any special instruction; and I have also experienced the magical effects of the Jew's harp in illnesses as well. Mineral magnetism is generally known; I need only indicate, in order to be understood, that the Jew's harp exercises its magnetic effect on the nerves in a similar manner. I have often been successful in gently resolving pain in feverish illnesses, nervous disturbances, and physical overstimulations through the tones of the instrument; I have calmed violent excitement and have induced sweet sleep in the restless by this means. The tones of the Jew's harp act by animal magnetism in patients so treated, especially by calming and soothing convulsive phenomena.

Every hearer will partly perceive this effect in order to confirm the truth of this statement for himself. I have demonstrated the most striking proofs of this magical effect not only with individual patients, but also before many witnesses. If the essence of the little instrument consists of simplicity, delicacy, natural purity, characteristic vibrations, and magnetic effect, it is easy to explain that it is seldom treated as a musical instrument; for in order to learn to understand such an essence, the learner or observer must have a sense of music and some knowledge of it. A certain delicacy of feeling which communicates itself to external treatment will also make learning the instrument simpler. Penetration into the nature of every essence is difficult and demands spirit!

With respect to the type of music for the little instrument, I will only permit myself to communicate my experiences, in the friendly hope of receiving many corrections and expansions of my remarks from connoisseurs of music. The Jew's harp is a monochord and contains only major tones. The steel tongue is stretched through the middle of the body of the iron (or silver or gold) bow like a string; it is moved by striking and sounds by means of the breath, just as the string of an aeolian harp does by means of a breeze. If one would speak of the Jew's harp as an instrument, then we must say that the mouth and oral cavity act as a sounding board, while the steel spring produces the vibrations, as does a string. In this way, the laws of the string and wind instruments operate together. Every Jew's harp has, aside from its fundamental tone, the third, fifth, seventh, octave, ninth, tenth, and, in the deeper ones, the twelfth—all clearly sounding; perhaps indifferently, the fifteenth and seventeenth.

The tones of an instrument whose fundamental tone is F, for example, are illustrated in the musical example on page 107, no. 1.

It is not possible to play melodies with only one Jew's harp: it is necessary to have at least two. These two instruments must be separated from each other by either a fourth or a fifth. If F is taken as the fundamental tone, the following are obtained at the interval of a fourth (see example no. 2). The first Jew's harp is above and the second, below.

If C is taken as the fundamental tone, the following notes are obtained at an interval of a fifth (see example no. 3). The second Jew's harp is *above*, the first, *below*. In pieces of music which remain mostly in the lower register, the fourth is necessary; in those which go higher, the fifth.

Although each individual Jew's harp produces only the harmonic triad, it is possible, with practice, to produce the second, fourth, and sixth in rapid passages by a pressure of the tongue against the palate (similar to that in the production of the sound *k*). It is always necessary, however, to begin and end on a note which really lies within the triad (see example no. 4).

In these examples, the Jew's harp is tuned in G and the hollow notes are those in continuity which are compensated for by the tongue-palate pressure. It is thus possible to descend in half-tones to the fundamental tone. The accomplished player strengthens the action of the tones by using two Jew's harps simultaneously, producing the accord in this way. An advantage of the instrument lies in the fact that one always hears the accord of the individual Jew's harp, regardless of the tone one strikes, according to one's desire; this creates the effect of a harmony and is simply, so to speak, the magical accompaniment of this instrument itself. The upper tone resembles a soft, but full, flute tone; the bass is attractively similar to the sound of a trombone, and the resonant tones of the accord, especially the fifth and octave, are occasionally perceived as ethereally echoing mediants. If the tones are known on one instrument, then they are known on all, because only the tuning of the accord is differently determined. As the pitch of this small instrument is very pure and it is almost impossible to make it yield an impure tone, it is among the most perfect instruments that we possess, especially when it has a somewhat louder sound. In order to give the professional musician an overview of the type of music for this instrument which he may use in composition, I note the accords of the instrument which I use for music. These are illustrated on plate 8.

My smaller Aura has twelve Jew's harps, of which I take six in each hand. The following fundamental tones are comprised on the right hand and the left hand (see no. 6).

My larger Aura has twenty Jew's harps, of which I take ten in each hand. The fundamental tones of these, for the right and left hands, are illustrated in no. 7.

If one wanted to increase the number of individual instruments and take twelve in each hand, this number, as Scheibler notes, would make the whole instrument very inconvenient and, because of the 192 tones which it would comprise, so difficult to learn that few would devote themselves to it. It is also neither possible to find Jew's harps which permit these ranges, nor does the construction of the human mouth allow the lowest and highest of twelve such variously tuned Jew's harps (twenty-four, in fact) to be made uniformly responsive.

VI. Introduction to Musical Use

Every art has its mysterious, unfathomable depths in the soul of an individual endowed by the muses. Outside these mysterious depths, and growing out of them, gaining space and developing, every art also has its craft, i.e., a component which may be learned and practiced, which must be learned and practiced!

Didaskalia, *Morgenblatt*, March 1830

1. PRELIMINARY REMARKS

Things are conquered only by submitting to them at the beginning.

—Bacon

There is no art in which theory seems to be weaker and more inadequate than music; for it is possible to understand all the rules and principles of music and still be an ordinary musician; on the other hand, it is possible to know very little theory and be a very good musician. Thus, there are only leading hints which can be given for technique, as music is the universal language of nature and each person may speak this language, like every other language, well or badly according to his character. But what makes the Jew's harp so difficult to learn is that one realizes the value of the instrument only after assiduous effort, and when one knows the instrument, its study never flatters one's vanity, as is the case with other instruments, which may be played under any constellation, because its use depends upon certain conditions of mood, company, place, and time. It may often appeal as a rarity, but just because of this it is frequently considered trivial, which it is not. As in all other studies, the person of independent mind possesses a rich treasure, which the mechanical individual, who only holds to the words and artifices of his teacher and agrees only with him, can never acquire. It is possible to awaken talent by application, but some gift must be present to assure true success. In addition to application, there must be physical qualities, inborn mental disposition for such efforts. If the soul is to be seized by an artistic perception, the soul must be attuned and predisposed to it: that is a well known view; the attunement of the soul, however, is not always at hand, like common things: it is produced by appropriate circumstances. The day scarcely admits this receptivity— our eyes disturb us too often, while the quiet evening induces more this quiet mood which is suitable for the instrument. If one is occupied continually with the instrument, it is noteworthy that the more familiar one becomes with it, the simpler it seems to the listener, who might think that no artistic training is required for it. But without a conscientiousness that extends to every detail, nothing of the sort may be accomplished.

2. PHYSICAL CHARACTER OF THE LEARNER

Le génie c'est la patience. [Genius consists of patience.]

—Buffon

The singer, like the musician who wishes to play wind instruments correctly, must have a particular physical character, without which neither one may accomplish anything genuine. The first must have all his vocal organs in a healthy condition; for the latter, it is not only the vocal organs, but the hands which must also be of suitable deftness. Both must have a healthy ear and an inborn ability to discriminate tones, which is termed a musical ear. The Jew's harp is an instrument for which the mechanics of singing and wind instrument playing must be united. It is therefore indispensable to explain the requisite physical character to the learner. When we speak of vocal organs, we understand those organs such as the larynx and its environment, the soft palate, the hyoid bone, etc., and the connected parts: oral cavity, teeth, tongue, trachea, and lungs. The voice is explained by the construction of the larynx.[8] The larynx is a conical pipe through which air resounds in the same manner as a bird-call. This voice pipe has all the necessary properities to permit the air enclosed in it, regardless of its small quantity, to produce various and even very deep tones. Its lower portion is constructed of elastic walls which may accommodate themselves to every degree of tension; while the mouth is more or less open, the spacious content of the air column may be varied thereby, which also has a marked effect on the number of vibrations. The extent to which the lips are separated from each other changes the voice pipe into either an almost open or almost closed conical pipe. The cartilaginous parts (carthilagines arytaenoideae) become narrow and wide through use, for all parts are elastic. The larynx, in which the voice is produced, descends and expands for deep tones, ascends and contracts for high ones. For that reason, basses lower their hands when singing, tenors raise theirs. But the larynx is not the only vocal organ. Above it lie various flexible organs which, together, comprise the oral cavity and an essential part of that wonderful musical instrument, the human voice.[9]

It has been known for a long time that although the vocal cords play the main role in producing the voice, other organs also contribute considerably in modifying its tone and loudness. The famous anatomist Fabricius ab Aquapendente demonstrated that the voice is produced in the larynx, after he had indicated the character of its ascending and descending, and consequently the lengthening and shortening of the oral cavity. He also describes the change in width which the organ undergoes in proceeding from a low tone to a high one. The soft palate essentially belongs to the vocal organs and forms a partition between the mouth and the nasal cavity. Composed of muscles, it is covered on its front surface with the mucous membrane of the mouth and on its back surface, facing the pharynx, with the mucous membranes of the nasal cavity and choana. It hangs from there like a curtain capable of manifold movement at the back edge of the palatine bone downward, supported on both sides by two skin-like folds, while the lowest twice-curved edge has a lengthened point in the middle, which is turned directly to the middle line of the tongue root. We find this soft palate structure, however, only where it is connected with the power of speech and the perfect articulation of tones and modulation of loudness, i.e., only in humans. As the soft palate is so important for the voice, the smallest opening in it or any significant loss of substance in its edges results in a decrease in the harmony of the voice. If there are greater disturbances of the soft palate or a congenital cleft palate, a total destruction of the characteristic harmony of the human voice occurs. The soft palate thus has a very important influence on the correct direction of tone, so that the tones are not pressed downward into the throat or upward into the nasal passages. With deep tones, the soft palate stretches upward and back, the uvula, which occupies the middle of the soft palate, is shortened (se replie sur elle même). With high tones, the situation is reversed: the soft palate is lowered, the larynx rises, the tonsils swell and come closer together. The tongue itself exercises a powerful influence on the modulation of tones, in that it is raised or lowered or is grooved into a channel, and in that way the hyoid bone is held firmly in a certain position when the larynx gives out a certain tone. When the larynx reaches the highest point in the series of tones, and its modulation occurs through its own movement, it seems to fix itself and then a new type of tone follows. Magistel's research has confirmed the old belief that the *nervus hypoglossus* and *glosso pharyngeus* serve in movement and are extremely important here. All that has been said here finds its full application in the study of the Jew's harp. The larynx, soft palate, tongue, tonsils—all these organs are mostly active in playing the Jew's harp. In the first months, when one begins to play the Jew's harp, the uvula and tonsils become inflamed. The tongue hurts. At the beginning, the tone drones so in the player's head that he becomes almost dazed; the teeth become numb and a tingling sensation is felt in them, like that in a limb that has fallen asleep. These sensations disappear with time and pleasant feelings take their place, similar to those which the glass harmonica brings about, i.e., the nerves are stimulated.

No less indispensable for the technique of the little instrument are requirements of ear and hand, the former to tune the instrument properly and to be able to master the tones correctly, the latter to manipulate the instrument gently and surely. Herodotus says: "The rational and divine part of human nature resides in the ear." This sense is alive under all temporal conditions; it is also more active than the sense of sight, and hence more inward. If I do not wish to see, then I turn my eyes aside; with the ear, this turning away is performed inwardly. The ear is more comprehensive, but can also exercise great discretion; for in a concert I can listen to the instrument that interests me: violin, flute, etc. The ear of the learner, then, must be suitably constructed. One might wish every learner and every hearer of the instrument a Beduin's ear. The Beduin Arab, with his wide, prominent, arched, flexible ear is endowed with very fine, sharp hearing. In the lonely desert, in the cool of the evening, his supple ears announce to him, hours distant, the tread of the camel, and, at unbelievable distances, the rushing of the spring. As the sense of hearing is so valuable for man, how useful it would be if he could support this sense with instruments and achieve what the telescope and the microscope achieve for the sense of sight, so that tones would be audible from far greater distances and would be distinguished with far greater precision. The amplification of tones, if there were such an instrument besides the ear-trumpet, would be highly appropriate for the Jew's harp. I have conducted several experiments along these lines and have found that even the hard of hearing can perceive the softest sounds, with deep emotion, with the aid of ear-trumpets. The sense must be trained for music in order to learn the Jew's harp successfully.

How important the hand and its physical character are for this instrument! If one considers the marvelous structure of the hand, its high perfection as a tool, how, by its language, it manifests itself as a servant of the spirit, then one cannot be surprised that Anaxagoras ascribes the superiority of man to the possession of his hand. In this perfection, the tool precisely corresponds to the higher spiritual level on which man stands, in that the hand is capable of accomplishing everything that man devises. In playing the Jew's harp, it must be strong and agile; stiff fingers, weakness or hardness of the hand would make it unsuited for this use.

Now if the vocal organs, the oral cavity, and the teeth are healthy, and the lungs are not particularly disturbed by the inhalations and exhalations, if the ear is not wholly untrained, and if the hand is talented, then the learner possesses all the necessary physical requirements. The Jew's harp player must avoid everything which can damage the voice or the vocal organs, especially. Astringent, fat, too bitter, or too sweet foods, as well as hot and sharp drinks, may harm the vocal organs. Nuts, almonds, baked goods, even milk, etc., cause a fat impurity in the throat which lasts for several hours. Tea spoils the voice; only pure water strengthens it. Becoming overheated or cold, as well as rapid changes of temperature, should be avoided. Heavy, warm air is detrimental, while cool, dry air in a not too enclosed space is the most beneficial. Nature has surrounded the throat with a moist film, hence a fine tone must be, so to speak, lush, i.e., it must be heard as full and free when it issues from the lips. Habits must be avoided; they are superfluous and a flaw in gracefulness, for in every movement of the body, the observer may find that fine line which draws attention to oneself by a sober grace and thus increases enjoyment.

3. POSTURE, TOUCH, ARTIFICES

> Manus autem esse videtur non unum instrumentum, sed multa.
> Est enim, ut ita loquar, instrumentum ante instrumenta!
>
> —Galenus

A decent posture is, generally in life, valuable and desirable, but it is indispensable here—one may take the word in its widest or narrowest sense. The musician is advised to pay attention to the posture of his whole body when performing a piece: the position of his head, his hands; he must not distort his features or his mouth, not gesticulate unnecessarily with his hands, but hold them firmly, so that any exertion will go unnoticed; no matter how difficult all this is, it is essential to maintain a good posture when playing the Jew's harp and makes the process much easier later. Correct calculation of breathing is included here, for if the breath fails at the wrong time, it is as though the spirit were departing. In any case, a great deal of breath is not required, but only its intelligent utilization. The hands are very important when playing, as they hold the instrument uniformly against the teeth; moving them too much and agitating the arms harms deportment. One may easily become aware of the indecency of such movements if one sees Jew's harp players who lay down one instrument and pick up another in the usual manner: the hands go to the table and imitate, so to speak, the movements of the hands when eating. The distinctive feature of posture with regard to the Jew's harp is the most difficult aspect of learning the instrument; for that reason, everything stated under section 3 is recommended to be followed in detail by the learner.

The instrument lies before me on the table (the best here is the rather large form, as illustrated in plate 1, no. 3): to pick it up, I place three fingers (of either hand)—the thumb, index, and middle fingers—in the form of a triangle whose point—my thumb—is toward me. In this manner (the triangle may be somewhat displaced), I place the instrument, after opening my lips a bit, against my slightly parted teeth, and I place my fourth finger, which has sufficient freedom and strength, on the tip of the Jew's harp's tongue. No other method is either possible or expedient. With this method, one may bring either one or two Jew's harps to the mouth for playing. A completely different method obtains with instruments which have two tongues or with the composite instrument called the Aura. The instrument with two tongues is lifted in the same way, but if the fourth finger is not able to reach the second tongue, then the fifth finger is used as well. The method with the Aura of twelve instruments, of which six are held in each hand, requires particular attention in changing the individual Jew's harps. The Aura is also lifted with the thumb, index, and middle fingers, by the handle which extends upright from the plate; when the instrument is placed against the mouth, the middle finger is released and the handle remains grasped by only the thumb and index finger, while the middle finger is left free to turn the instrument to whatever point is required. The fourth finger reaches the tips of all the tongues comfortably, in order to move them. The experienced player also uses the fifth finger when it is convenient for him to do so. The method of holding an Aura of twenty instruments, i.e., ten in each hand, is more difficult, but practice and familiarity make everything easier. The instrument is also lifted by the thumb and index finger, but the middle finger must support them in order to hold it firmly to the teeth, while the fourth finger helps to press it and the fifth finger reaches the tongue tips to move them (see plate 5). After achieving steadiness in this way, the thumb and index finger eventually become adequate and the third and fourth fingers are used for pressure and for turning the instrument. It is, however, always the fifth finger that is used for moving the tongues, due to the large circumference of the plate.

When an individual Jew's harp is held lightly but firmly against the teeth, the fourth finger strikes downward on the small rounded part of the tongue. This finger, which is extended a bit crookedly, must be flicked straight ahead: the tongue is set into movement in this way. Lifting the tongue is detrimental to the instrument and is contrary to the laws of mechanics. The Aura with six instruments for each hand is struck in the same way with the fourth finger; with the ten-instrument Aura, the fifth finger does the striking. When the tongue of the Jew's harp is brought into motion by striking, the tones are produced by a gentle breathing, during which the mouth, tongue, larynx—the vocal organs generally—are used as in whistling. A certain skill and experience quickly teach the manner of producing an attractive tone.

Artifices may be described and can be useful to the learner, but everyone attains his own artifices through experiment after he has become acquainted with his instrument. Most Jew's harp players play on two instruments simultaneously, yet every musician knows that there are few melodies without changeovers to other keys; the player must thus put down at least one Jew's harp and lift another or frequently change instruments, as described above. The composition of the Aura, as accomplished by my honored friend, H. Scheibler, does away with this inconvenience. Through this device of combining many small instruments into a whole, it is now possible also to produce minor scales. It is a considerable help in learning the Jew's harp that one need not rely simply on one's musical ear, but must be aware of the rigid rules and learn to practice them. First of all, it is necessary to learn from written notes. In writing notation for the Jew's harp, I always mark the Jew's harp which the player must take with a quarter or half note which has a descending line, while the melody is marked with notes where the lines ascend (plate 9). There are many examples of this in the appended musical examples. The notes with strokes through them are produced on the same Jew's harp as those occurring near them without strokes by means of a palatal pressure, similar to that used to produce a slight k sound (see plate 9, the example marked K). They are called continuous notes and have already been discussed under the rubric "Type of Music." If such continuous notes do not have a stroke through them, they are breathed or glided over without using the k palatal pressure: see the f in example B. For breathing practice, example C is given, where notes which must be produced with a new breath are marked with the sign M. Staccato (checking the tones with the lips) is marked with short strokes (see example D in the Écossaise). If two Jew's harps are held at the mouth simultaneously, the notes for the one are written on top and, for the other, on the bottom. The notes for the right-hand instrument are usually written on top, while those on the bottom are for the left-hand instrument. This is presented in example E. Surprisingly enough, the Jew's harp contains tones which lie below the fundamental tone; it is almost impossible to explain in words how such notes are produced.

It may perhaps help those who learn the instrument by means of a written text to know that if one begins with these deep notes, the slight k is used and the following notes are treated as though they were really capable of being produced by the Jew's harp (example F in the Waltz, plate 9, teaches this). If one proceeds from the fundamental tone to the deeper triad, the next notes below that are treated as though they were actually in the Jew's harp, so that E-flat in example G (see the Waltz) and the following are produced by the k pressure. The C here is produced by the k pressure after the E-flat is treated as being actually present. If one proceeds deeper below the fundamental tone by an intermediary note, this is produced by the k pressure and the next is treated as present (see example H in the Waltz, where the G is produced by the *k* pressure and the E-flat is assumed to be present.). The Jew's harp is tuned in A-flat for examples A, F, G, and H.

This is sufficient to indicate the artifices whose use will be brought to artistic proficiency through experience and will yield satisfaction and pleasure.

4. ONE INSTRUMENT, TWO INSTRUMENTS, THE AURA

> The simpler the means, the more worthy of amazement is the success.

In order to put the rules given above into practice, one first obtains a Jew's harp, makes attempts at holding and striking it, learns to use one's breath and one's vocal organs. The learner who is also musical will obviously progress more rapidly than one who is studying the elements of music for the first time with the instrument. When the Jew's harp has been lifted in the correct manner and the method of holding it is understood, then striking is attempted and an effort is made to produce a tone by breathing. The first tone to be sought is the fundamental tone in which the instrument is tuned. One must be able to produce this fundamental tone firmly and with assurance. One next proceeds to the third, fifth, and octave, and the harmony is practiced until one is sure of it. When one can produce one harmony, then, as it were, one knows them all, in that every Jew's harp has the same range, and one cannot fail once one has mastered these exercises with one harmony. All the instructions given in section 3 should be practiced on one instrument, paying attention to the physical requirements (see section 2). As one is able to produce a melody only with two Jew's harps, one will soon wish to use two instruments for one's own pleasure. Now begins the difficult stage of study, for all of a sudden in striking, a jangling results; the breath fails and one does not know how to lead the tones from one Jew's harp to the other. With a little diligence, however, it becomes clear very soon; for after knowing the harmonies of every Jew's harp, the trained ear gives assistance and the hesitant tones become more flowing and sound more pleasant. The truly moving singing of the instrument encourages diligence and reward follows. As it is not possible to produce a melody with less than two instruments, these instruments must be tuned a fourth or a fifth distant from each other, as mentioned above. At a distance of a fourth, the higher one has the fundamental tone; at a fifth, the lower one. Changeovers from one key to another have been facilitated by Scheibler's arrangement of the Aura, and by means of these fourths and fifths one can make whatever composition one likes. After a certain degree of practice, an Aura should be assembled, in order to avoid the burdensome and ungraceful lifting and putting down of the individual Jew's harps.

5. SELECTION, IMPROVEMENT, TUNING

> Trivial things are also often of the greatest importance in life;
> for that reason, one should not ignore their requirements. One
> can develop a great deal of skill through trivia.

In case it is inconvenient to buy this very cheap instrument by the dozen, which is actually the most expedient method, the merchant will permit selection if he is given a higher price, as the ordinary customer seeks one characteristic in the instrument—which certainly remains after a selection—namely, very rigid tongues, which are unsuitable for musical use. The clarity of the instrument may be recognized by the fact that it produces the octave, ninth, tenth, and, in deep Jew's harps, the twelfth, easily and without incidental sounds; uniformity consists in the fact that the rigid tongues do not produce sounds which are too loud and the lax ones, tones that are too soft. Too great a variation in the tongues produces a poor action. When I make my selection, I always have several dozen iron instruments in front of me and try them for tongue vibration, clarity, and uniformity in tone production and strength. Jew's harps which yield incidental sounds or which jangle, I immediately discard, unless they are affected by dust or dirt. I make sure that the instrument has not been made in too clumsy a fashion and that it is not raw or fissured, and especially that unevennesses can be polished out easily. I see to it that the springs are not too rigid, that they are more yellowish than blue in color, and that they are firmly attached to the back of the frame. I consider that the broad springs having such qualities are the best. The upright part of the spring must not be too thin, but hard and somewhat rounded, rather than flat. The clarity of the instrument is dependent upon whether the two cuts of the tongue stand absolutely parallel to the opposite angles of the instrument's frame.

The Jew's harp must not be too thick at the back and not too broad or yet too thin at the end that is placed against the teeth. Some must sound high, others low, without any tuning; these are easily found. There are some Jew's harps which do not withstand vibrations, others which are unclear in the high notes; both types should not be used.

It is possible to correct small defects, but the correction takes so much time that it is better to find another Jew's harp. If, for example, there are small blemishes on an otherwise exceptionally good instrument, these may be polished down on a rotating stone without harming the instrument; filing is deleterious because it jolts the spring too much. If the two cuts of the tongue do not stand completely parallel to the frame, a careful bending of the spring in the appropriate direction will set things to rights. If the upright part of the tongue is bent, but not ruined, the defect can be corrected with a small pair of pliers. If the frame of the Jew's harp is bent and bending the tongue does not help, then the instrument is unusable.

In instruments of my design (see plate 3), if the tongue is damaged, it is unscrewed and the instrument fitted with a suitable replacement.

Once I have selected good Jew's harps in this manner and corrected their small defects, I use shellac to make tiny balls, some as small as a grain of millet, and affix these to each instrument. My purpose is, first, because the finger glides more easily over the upright tip of the tongue and movement is facilitated, while striking is more uniformly accomplished; secondly, a raw instrument, even if it has the correct fundamental tone, never sounds as gentle as one with a tiny ball attached, but always somewhat sharp. According to the proportions of the higher or lower tones, the tips of the tongues will now have very small or considerably larger balls attached to them. According to Heinrich Scheibler's ingenious invention, the Jew's harps are tuned by the following method: a guitar is tuned in the key of G-major by means of a tuning fork, next the Jew's harp in G is tuned, the *capo d'astro* is attached, and tuning proceeds in this simple manner. Tuning in various tones is indicated by selecting for the higher tones those Jew's harps which have come from the maker sounding higher, and for the lower ones, those sounding lower. It may be necessary to either reduce or increase the size of the small shellac balls on the tips of the tongues; the latter is accomplished by softening shellac with the aid of a wax candle. Reducing the size is done with a small file, such as those used by watchmakers, and requires much patience, care, frequent striking to test the tone—and a fine ear! It is easy to build up the small balls on the tongue tip: a small amount of shellac is applied to the tongue and the Jew's harp is rapidly turned in a circular motion in the air. It is also possible to tune the instruments just as clearly by means of a well-tempered piano. Aside from handling and striking, tuning is the most difficult process in learning the instrument. But in tuning any instrument, just as with the Jew's harp, there is a sure test of whether the instrument is in tune: if one listens carefully to the sound of two Jew's harps struck in unison, there should be no incidental sound, no variation in tone, but the two tones should sound together as one.

6. MAINTENANCE OF THE INSTRUMENT

What man achieves by his exertions is dear to him; what he grows to love and value, he also wants to keep.

If one wants to keep good instruments undamaged, they must never be let out of one's hands, as usually the listener wants to touch the instrument or even try it. Such trials always end badly, and one should always have a couple of similar instruments to give away. The greatest enemy of the instrument is rust, as the whole instrument is usually made of iron, and the tongue must be of iron even if the frame is made of silver, gold, or other noble metals. Rusting is hindered by treating it in the following manner: after the instrument has been made as smooth as possible by polishing, the places which are touched by the breath are painted, by means of a fine artist's brush, with clear amber varnish, which is then permitted to dry on a warm oven. The whole spring of the Jew's harp should not be varnished, as this harms the tone; the varnish should also be very thin, or else the tone becomes too dull, placing it against the lips and tongue is unpleasant, and the varnish flakes off. It is also possible to prevent rusting by cold plating with gold, which covers both the tongue and the frame of the instrument. In both ways, the aim will be achieved.

The instrument should be carefully guarded from falling, as the tongue may be bent or even broken if this happens.

Incorrect or violent striking also ruins the instrument's tongue and should be avoided; I have had Jew's harp tongues break during playing as a result of this. To maintain them, the instruments must be kept in such a way that the tongues always lie free and do not suffer through pressure or impact during transport. This is best accomplished with small cases in which the frame lies so high that the tongues, turned downward, do not reach the bottom of the case. The Aura, or composite instrument, is fixed in such a way by screws that damage can result only from harsh treatment when screwing it together. The instruments become better with use: reason enough to maintain them carefully.

7. ARRANGEMENTS

The greatest art is to be able to conceal art!

In arrangements, everything must be united that one can think of, which could not be arranged in any other way. If this is not always possible to achieve, at least the expedient may certainly be arrived at. My honored friend, Heinrich Scheibler, after first hearing the exquisitely beautiful, truly moving sound—as he himself expressed it—felt induced to think of a means to overcome the instrument's imperfection and to unite several instrument, as it is seldom possible to sustain a melody with two Jew's harps. It must be admitted that he was extremely successful. In the *Allgemeine musikalische Zeitung,* no. 30, 24 July 1816, he made known an arrangement of instruments which, however, was vastly superseded by his later version, which I will describe here; he thereby raised the otherwise disdained Jew's harp to the rank of musical instruments. The Aura arrangement, by which I can take six Jew's harps in each hand, and which I greatly enjoy using, consists of two small, round, lacquered sheet-metal discs with a diameter of 2⅛ rheinisch Zoll [1 Zoll = 1 inch]. On the disc which is placed underneath, divided by gold lines into six areas having various colors, the fundamental tones of the individual Jew's harps are written in black or gold; the upper disc is smooth. Both discs are lined with velvet. Between these is a round wooden core, made of plum-tree wood, which has a diameter of 1¼ Zoll. On this wooden disc, which is barely ⅛ Zoll thick, there lies a brass disc, cut into six parts, but placed together to form a disc, each of whose parts is fastened to the wooden disc by a small pin. These individual pieces of the brass disc have small holes on their periphery, through which each Jew's harp is tied so tightly with black silk, by the end where the tongue is attached, that the instruments' tongues remain completely untouched. Through both these lacquered discs, as well as through the brass and wooden discs, there runs a screw thread. Into this, at the top, an upright brass machined pin or bolt is screwed, which extends out at the bottom for the purpose of screwing into a round velvet-lined case, if desired. The individual instruments are now in place around these discs, their tongues upright and facing outward; they are covered top and bottom at the point where the tongues are attached to the frames by the ⅛-Zoll discs. The diameter of the circle constructed by the six Jew's harps is 4⅝ Zoll. When playing, each hand holds such an apparatus.

The largest Aura arrangement which is possible for the human mouth and hand consists of ten individual Jew's harps for each hand, so that twenty different instruments may be alternated in the course of playing.

Plate 4, no. 1, shows a general view of one such Aura, i.e., the instrument for one hand; one of the same type is held in the other hand. The sheet-metal disc is lacquered green and lined with gold and green velvet, which is visible through the pierced upper disc. The individual Jew's harps are of the type illustrated in plate 1, no. 4. The diameter of the circle described by the apparatus with all instruments is 7 Zoll. The combined weight of the apparatus for each hand is 12 Loth ½ Quentchen, Berlin weight [1 Loth = 10 grams; 1 Quentchen = 1.772 grams]. Several parts of the apparatus are presented on the same plate. No. 2*a* shows the brass handle in actual size; *b* shows the screw which runs through the two discs and into which the handle is screwed; no. 3*a* shows the screw which runs through the middle of all the discs to hold them together; *b* is the steel lamella through which the screw runs on the upper disc—it serves to help hold it firmly; *c* is the brass nut on the lower disc through which the middle screw runs, to extend enough in order to attach the instrument to a suitable round case in which it may be transported without damage.

Plate 5 shows a view of how the instrument is held and the tongues struck with the fifth finger (the left hand is holding the instrument).

Plate 6 shows both lower discs of the apparatuses, which are lacquered in color and gold. The letters are the fundamental tones of the Jew's harps, which are indicated with points.

Plate 7 contains the most important part of the apparatus in actual size, as in all the plates. No. 1 shows the upper part of the inner plate. The brown disc is made of hardwood and serves as a sounding-board; the silver-colored circle and the triangle are made of sheet-metal. No. 2 gives a view of the underside of the inner plate. The sheet-metal ring is attached to the wooden disc with small steel screws; it serves as a cushion which firmly holds the individual triangles to which the Jew's harps are soldered. The placement of the instruments is also shown. No. 3 represents an individual Jew's harp soldered to sheet-metal.

It is evident from this how simple and ingenious Scheibler's apparatus is, and how it is possible to take all twenty Jew's harps out of the apparatus in one minute and replace them all in the same length of time, and thus how easily a damaged Jew's harp may be replaced by a good one.

Plate 8 shows in examples the rules described in section 3.

Plate 9 contains several pieces of music for the Aura, some with guitar accompaniment.

The following items are required for the procedures described in the foregoing text:

a) For selection: a ruler and a compass.
b) For tuning: leather covered cleaning rods, shellac, a small file, a small pair of pliers such as those used by watchmakers, and an equally small vise.
c) For maintenance: amber varnish or gold for cold plating, a paintbrush, small brushes.

A small notebook to contain pieces of music written for the Aura.

A case measuring 7¾ Zoll high by 10 Zoll wide by 9⅛ Zoll long will contain all these items, apparatuses, and miscellaneous things securely and elegantly.

A finely produced little book to record the autograph signatures and comments of those who have heard the Aura easily serves as a souvenir of many pleasant hours spent with close and respected friends.

VII. The Artist

A push of his finger
And all these bells

Give out a sweet sound
Finer than any harp;
No bird above
Or maiden in the sea
Can give out such
A song as his wife's.
Das Wunderhorn

Whoever wishes to be a proper human being and an artist must try to acquire this higher happiness through a continual overcoming of discomfort, but the fact is that an indefatigable quest for the beautiful, for a clear, true perception, a loving tending and conservation, is seldom encountered among people. For that reason, the true artist is such a rare phenomenon. Training for art demands a particular constellation of life, a particular stimulus, and a special natural receptivity for the given object.

Artistry may well be attained, but art, as the classic aspiration of the individual's life, stands too high for it to become common property; the wreath crowns only the gifted. Art proceeds with courageous strength along the open road of life, yet reaches the depths with every step. Its riches give joy to the highly educated, to the wise, and they delight the pure mind of ordinary people. It raises the common man above the vulgar and it permits the educated to perceive the divine strength in man!

The above motto realizes its full significance when applied to the modest Jew's harp if an artist places the instrument of delight—as Jean Paul calls it—against his lips and begins to draw the loveliest sounds that ever flowed over human lips, as consonant with the soul, from the living metal. Correct taste, discrimination, and judgment, however, must be cultivated and formed in man. As this is certainly true, the artist who wishes to produce his little instrument must wait for the proper moment, and it is surely excusable if he does not want to play at just any time or in any mood. The time is always right for ordinary things, but an artistic performance is nothing if it is not in the right place with the right lighting.

The first skilled player whom I heard was a certain Mauriska (a Bohemian?), who performed a few selections from Pleyel's compositions and, in the quiet evening hours, aroused astonishment in his listeners. I was then at the beginning of my musical formation and I recall having heard rare and marvelously pure tones. I later heard "good Koch," as Jean Paul called him—a modest retired soldier who used to travel around with his instruments. In a letter of 19 January 1784, Schiller writes from Mannheim to Zumsteeg: "Your Jew's harp virtuoso has been given protection through the conductor, Franzel." Thus, he was touring even then and was, as far as is known, the first to appear as an artist before the public. He had the good fortune to have his art praised by the pen of a Jean Paul and his name honorably known to posterity. In later years I was visited by this modest man whose gift was due to his fine ear, as he had not been able to attain to any musical training, and he was delighted at the perfection which the gentle instrument had attained.

> What rings out from the heights of heaven,[10]
> Beautifully soft, like a ghostly song,
> Contained by a star, drawn from star to star
> Through the wide space of the twilight?
>
> Is it the sound of swan's wings waving,
> Quivering down on moonbeams,
> And echoing from far-off rocky hills as it
> Floats on the gentle movement of the evening breeze?
>
> Is it lutes from times long past,
> Gliding down from azure mountain heights
> Softly in the mild rustling of the evening,
> Wafting longing into my breast?
>
> Is it sighs, love's yearning
> Gently dipped in dew and flowers' scent—
> Like the echoing sounds of flute notes,
> Whispering of dim distances through the twilight?
>
> But listen, twelve bell peals ring out
> And wake the melancholy of faint laments,
> And holy showers break forth from silent tombs
> Through the gloom of night!
>
> Voices of presentiment call through the silence
> And the stars burn more brightly—
> Over the tones of angelic harps
> Holy spirits shiningly ascend to heaven!
>
> —Arminia

With a sure awareness of his knowledge of the instrument, in 1816 I heard Dr. Cosmeli (from Pless in Silesia), well-known through his travels and his command of languages. He played on six individual Jew's harps, rejecting any assembly of them as inhibitory, and as a skillful flutist, it was to be expected that he had correctly grasped the method of the instrument. He delighted me in my happy household with his marvelous sounds, and as he gave me his views on his playing, he aroused the wish in me for a precise knowledge of the little instrument. I express my thanks to him in the lines which follow, and I have still kept the single Jew's harp with which I made my first attempts. I must say that the tones of my Aura often carry me to the homeland and their echoing sounds call to wakefulness the long past melodies of the soul.

Is this the wondrous lamenting of spirits?
Is this the soul's speech that is resounding?
They are like the tones of the aeolian harp,
Which penetrate the heart so mysteriously!

I do not know how it has happened,
What feeling has been wrung from my breast.
Your breath brings life even to iron.
Thus can an artist understand nature!

To freely command with hidden strength,
And to accomplish what no one would believe,
Has been given to you by the gods' favor.

You can, therefore, continue freely;
What you have gained can never be taken from you:
Your rich life, your serene art!

Franz Xaver Gebauer (conductor in the Augustiner-Hofpfarrkirche in Vienna) was supposed to have played the Jew's harp with wonderful skill. I visited him in Vienna, but had the misfortune not to find him at home. Unfortunately, he died young, on 13 January 1823. Among those who toured with the instrument in order to give concerts, I have frequently heard the two names Teichmüller and Eulenstein (from Heilbronn in Swabia); I have not met either of them, however. Teichmüller, who is also a portrait painter, is indebted to my friend Scheibler—although the latter is not musically trained—for much advice, and has received a great deal of acclaim and profit from his playing. The *Zeitung für die elegante Welt*, no. 115, 16 June 1826, and the *Morgenblatt*, no. 240, October 1826, have several reviews of the Jew's harp artist Eulenstein, who is also musically trained. The minister Zuckernegel (from near Breslau) frequently played on several Jew's harps at gatherings in the residence of the well-known Prince Blücher von Wahlstadt and pleased his hearers, although he was hardly a master of his instrument, as I may judge from having heard him. The actor Nahbel was also supposed to have played the Jew's harp skillfully, as I have been told. In Limburg an der Lahn, Kuhnert found an innkeeper and his sister who played the instrument, the sister handling it very delicately. This woman is perhaps the first to play the Jew's harp, yet it is so suitable for gentle feminine handling.

There may still be several[11] who play the instrument in quiet evening hours, whose success is unknown to me, but whose views and method it would be pleasant for me to know. The Tyroleans play the instrument in the usual manner, as far as I am aware, and the art-loving public of Berlin have been able to hear and judge their accomplishments on several occasions.

I include the musician Kunert (from Kauniz in Bohemia) among the skillful players of the Jew's harp. He was directed to me at the beginning of his artistic tour; he gave his first concert in Warmbrunn, in the Silesian mountains, and gave pleasure to everyone. He traveled throughout all of Germany, and the newspapers wrote a great deal about him and praised him, as did the May 1828 issue of the *Berlin-Vöss'sche Zeitung*. Although he played on individual instruments, changing them by lifting them and putting them down, which is always disturbing, his artistic accomplishments on the Jew's harp pleased me most of all. May the little instrument yet win him much friendly acclaim and thanks!

As an artist who has fully understood the essence of the instrument and played it masterfully, thanks to the highly ingenious method of assembling individual instruments, thus bringing them to perfection and raising them unquestionably to the level of a musical instrument, Heinrich Scheibler is worthy of note. With this greeting, I may perhaps best describe how the inner echo of his Aura tones are constantly reawakened in me:

> What is it that fills my ear so magically,
>   And brings the spirit deep inside?
>   It is a man whose gentle voice sings,
> From whose breast the world of tones springs forth!
>
> The marvelous is veiled in wonderous ways;
>   Here is a tone and yet a song that rings,
>   That calls like an echo from afar,
> Like ghostly senses that still your longing!
>
> But to describe it, to grasp it in words,
>   Is too difficult for most on earth.
>   Beauty fills the soul with bliss;
>
> I feel it all around; I leave description:
>   Such tones are like pearls,
>   A ghostly greeting that draws from soul to soul!
>
>
> What good friends people find on earth
>   When similar taste for art moves their hearts!
>   Could I, like you, set free the sweet sound
>   Which your Aura bears hidden in itself?
>
> Now I can state in silent wistfulness alone ,
>   What once I cried, moved by your sound!
>   Our coming and going is a dream!
>   The singer lies in a silent grave.[12]
>
> You breathed sweetly with your gentle tones
>   Delight into the heart through the intoxicated ear,
>   And beckoned to the world of magic.

This is the greatest reward of eternal beauty:
    Art draws the artist upward;
    I will only be your distant echo!

VIII. Comparisons

As the pineapple is a Pandora among fruits, so is the Aura a
Pandora among instruments.

The human voice is, as it were, the principle and ideal of instrumental
music; thus it may be explained that the human voice can imitate so
strikingly a great many instruments. The double relation of voice to
instrument and instrument to voice perhaps makes it possible for the
Jew's harp to contain the sounds of so many instruments. The tone
begins in the deep, beautiful bass of the trombone; next the joyful
sounds of the trumpet resound, accompanied by the controlled sound of
the horn; then the flute begins the melody, led from the fundamental
tone of the bassoon; the pipes of Pan throw in pearly notes; the sistrum
rustles to the middle tones of the tibia; a few triangle sounds finally call
through the dying echo notes of the aeolian harp.[13] That it is truly so,
every hearer may be convinced; yes, as mentioned above, the laws of the
string and wind instruments are united in the Jew's harp. The characteristic wonderful stimulation of the instrument surely lies also in its
relationship with many instruments. The long sounds which die away
have been unfittingly compared with the swan songs heard by our
ancestors, ridiculed by their descendants, and in our time again brought
out as well-founded. The song[14] of the swans in the long, dark winter
nights, when they pass through the air in flocks, is the most beautiful
thing that can be heard. One swan may suddenly start singing, the
length of a breath; then, after a small pause, another begins, as though
they are replying to each other. Aside from the sweetness of the tone
itself, the drawing out of one and the same tone by the singer in a
lingering fashion, waxing and waning, is of extraordinary beauty.

It has happened to me that in certain cases the Jew's harp resembles
the sound of a very gently played violin or *viole de fer*. Strikingly, although far more delicately, it sounds like the trumscheit, whose initial
buzzing tone is perceived like that of the Jew's harp.[15]

If one wishes to have another instrument accompany the Aura, the
guitar or zither appear to be the most suitable due to their lighter mood,
as the Tyroleans already use them. A delicately played and well-tuned
piano might perhaps also give pleasure to listeners in conjunction with
the Aura. The reader so inclined will find suitable pieces of music for
such endeavors.

What has been said seems to me sufficient for the person who considers that the Jew's harp is worthy of his close attention. Whoever wishes to learn it must not omit the basic rules in small print. Every teacher who has heard the Jew's harp once will at least be able to extract from these pages a method of judging the instrument. The deeper connoisseur of music may perhaps be induced to communicate his knowledge and advice in order to correct shortcomings, and thus cause the imperfect to become more perfect.

Notes

1. I refer to the following interesting work: "Der physikalische und musikalische Tonmesser, welcher durch den Pendel, dem Auge sichtbar, die absoluten Vibrationen der Töne, der Hauptgattungen von Combinations-Tönen, so wie die schärfste Genauigkeit gleichschwebender und mathematische Accorde beweist, erfunden und ausgeführt von Heinrich Scheibler, Seidenwaaren-Manufacturist in Crefeld. Nebst 3 Steindrucktafeln." (Essen: bei G. D. Bädeker, 1834).

2. I have thus fulfilled my promise. See *Zeitung für die elegante Welt* (Thursday, 5 October 1826); *Journal fur Literatur, Kunst, Luxus und Mode* 85 (St. Schutze, Weimar, 24 October 1826).

3. See his *Aesthetik der Tonkunst.*

4. See his *Hesperus,* Part 3, 3rd ed. (Berlin: Reimer, 1819), 100–110.

5. See the article "τὸ κρέμβαλον" in the *Basler Thesaurus* of 1577.

6. See "Notice sur l'art de fabriquer les guimbardes," communiqué à la Société d'encouragement par M. Baillet, Ingénieur en Chef des Mines, dans le *Bulletin de la Société d'encouragement pour l'industrie nationale,* 5e année (Paris, 1806), 101 [Translated elsewhere in this volume—TRANS.].

7. The Aure valley in the Pyrenees has its name from the mild south wind, the Aura, which blows every day at certain times.

8. See "Über die menschliche Stimme von Felix Savart". *Notizen aus dem Gebiete der Natur und Heilkunde von Froriep* 13:6 (February 1826).

9. Meyer's *Anatomische Darstellung der Stimmwerkzeuge* gives the best illustration. "Über das Gaumensegel des Menschen und der Säugethiere von J. F. Dieffenbach, Professor in Berlin." See *Heckers Annalen* (March 1826). Carl Heinrich Dzondzi: *Die Funktion des weichen Gaumens . . .* Mit 11 Abbildungen (Halle: C. A. Schwetschki und Sohn, 1831). Dr. Fr. Bennati (physician to the Italian Opera in Paris and himself a singer, deceased): *Sur le mecanisme et sur les maladies de la voix humaine.* Paris. Translated: *Über•die physiologischen und pathologischen Verhältnisse der menschlichen Stimme, ihre krankhaften Zustände und die Beseitigung derselben. Für Ärzte und Sänger.* Mit 3 Kpfrn: 8° (Leipzig? 1833 16 gGr.).

10. This poem was composed in 1816 after Koch's concert in Warmbrunn. *Vöss'sche Berliner Zeitung* (Thursday, 26 February 1818). A concert for contrabassoon, played by chamber musician Belke, and Jew's harp, played by Koch. The largest and smallest instruments played with the mouth, performed by two masters: this concert may only be called unique.

11. Herr Pulvermacher in Breslau has surely not given up the instrument? Does Herr Rigal in Paris still occasionally remove the instrument from its beautiful rose-embroidered case?

12. My friend died on 30 November 1837.

13. In terms of extremes, speaking of the aeolian harp, one thinks of the giant

harp of the Abbe Gattoni in Milan and of the Jew's harp, which can be held in the hollow of one's hand.

14. George Stewart Mackenzie's *Journey Through the Island of Iceland in the Year 1810.*

15. The *Trompeter-Marine, Trompeten-Geige,* or *Trumscheit* is a triangular bowed instrument invented by a Bohemian abbot. It has a long neck and a single string, which rests on a bridge; the string is touched with the finger while being bowed. It is, then, a monochord. The fingerboard is 6 Zoll long. An accomplished player can imitate the most disparate instruments in the narrow compass of the tonal development.

Plate 1   Pla

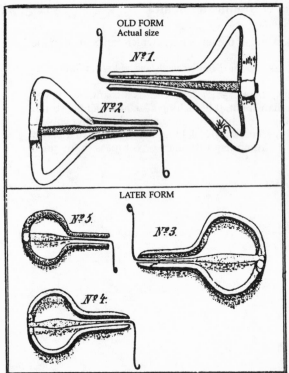
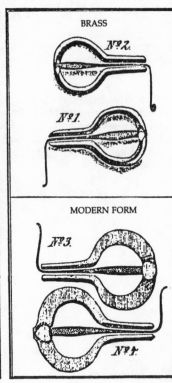

Plate 3

INSTRUMENTS ACCORDING TO DR. SCHMIDT'S
DESIGN

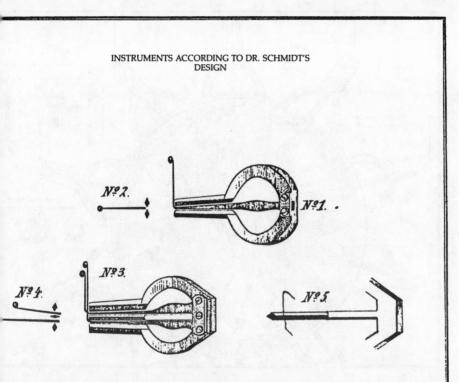

131

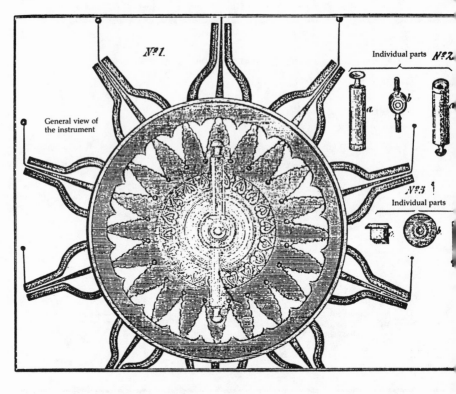

№1.

General view of
the instrument

Individual parts №2.

a.   b.

№3

Individual parts

Plate 5

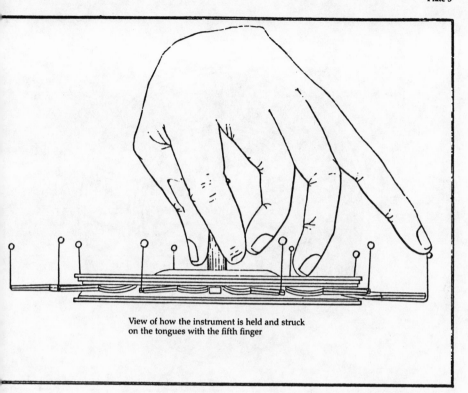

View of how the instrument is held and struck
on the tongues with the fifth finger

Plate 6

Bottom view of
the instrument

Right hand

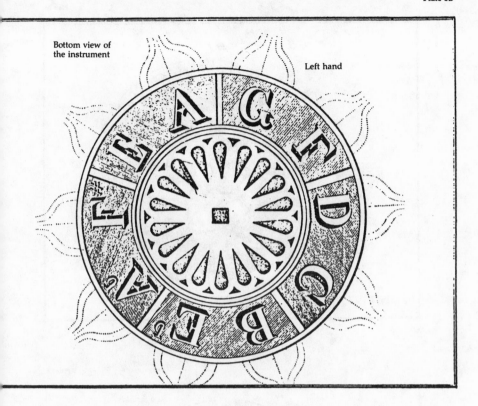

Bottom view of
the instrument

Left hand

135

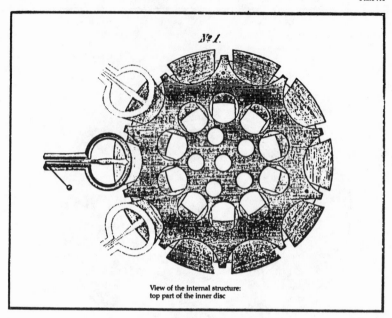

View of the internal structure:
top part of the inner disc

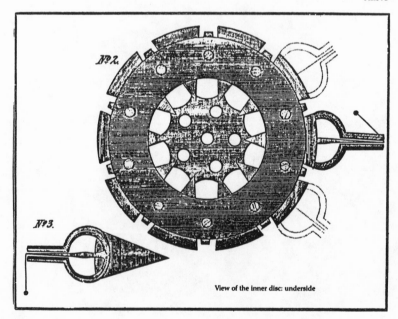

View of the inner disc: underside

1.

Aura with twelve Jew's harps

Pitches of the twelve Jew's harps

2.

Aura with twenty Jew's harps

Aura with twenty Jew's harps

Pitches of the twenty Jew's harps

Plate 9 for section 3 of the text

Explanation

In both these examples the learner will find the individual Jew's harps that he needs for each measure indicated by a quarter note with a line through it. For the sake of clarity, one may also make use of the half notes in this way. If both Jew's harps are to remain at the mouth, the notation for one is written above, for the other, below, as in example E.

A. Shows the continuous notes with lines through them; these are produced with the palatal pressure *k*.

B. Here, the F is a continuous note which is only breathed; it should be glided over without palatal pressure.

C. The sign *M* is given as an example for breathing.

D. The points . . . indicate staccato.

E. An example of notation when 2 Jew's harps are used at the same time.

F. Indicates the tones below the fundamental tone; the C is produced with palatal pressure, the following ones are treated as being available.

G. Indicates the descent from the fundamental tone in a triad; the first is treated as though it were really available, but the C is produced with palatal pressure.

H. Indicates descent from the fundamental tone with a continuous tone in between; this G is produced with palatal pressure, the following, as though they were available.

8.

Menuet aus Don Juan von Mozart.

Mich fliehen alle Freuden. Paisiello.

Vien qua Dorina bella.

Cherubini?

Fine.

Da Capo? al Fine

Wie sie so sanft ruhn.

Denkst Du daran!

V.S.

147

12.

Schlaf mein Prinzel etc.

Choral. Vom Himmel hoch.

14.

Choral. Wach auf mein Herz.

Musikstücke mit Begleitung d. Guitarre.

Liebes Mädchen hör:

150

Mennet. Mozart.

V.S.

Franz Paula Koch, the Jew's Harp Player

A. KAHLERT

THE JEW'S HARP [Kahlert uses the elegant term *Mundharmonika* "mouth-harmonica"—TRANS.] (Aura, Brummeisen, Maultrommel, Trombe), whose special charm the world has learned only during the past fifty years, has been most correctly described in its essence by Gottfried Weber (see *Cäcilia*, vol. 4, p. 49 [omitted from this anthology because the material comprised in it is presented in a more comprehensive manner by other works which have been included here—TRANS.], but the man who first brought this insignificant, long-despised instrument to a position of respect, at least in Germany, is mentioned there only in passing. Many people living in Germany undoubtedly remember him still: Franz Paula Koch—a virtuoso. May these lines contribute to keeping his memory alive.

This man's life was remarkable in many respects. Information is available about his destiny: *Kochs Biographie* by G. D. Geissler (Augsburg, 1793) and Schummel's *Breslauer Almanach* (Breslau, 1830, p. 258); finally, there is a manuscript source which will be more precisely specified below.

Jean Paul (*Hesperus* 2, p. 363) remembers him with enthusiasm and has erected a monument to him thereby which many virtuosi who appear with clamor and glitter might well wish for in vain.

Franz Paula Koch was born in 1761 in Mittersil, Salzburg. His parents appear to have been poor. He learned the bookbinding trade and, after his years of apprenticeship, he wandered through Austria and Bavaria.

It is uncertain whether he had any musical instruction in his youth; indeed, it is doubtful, as Koch's later musical achievements may be considered to be the result of self-instruction. In 1782, an incident occurred which would be decisive for the course of his whole life. In Regensburg he fell into the hands of Prussian recruiting officers, who liked his personality, and became (willingly or not) a Prussian soldier.

From *Neue Zeitschrift für Musik*, nos. 51 and 52, 26 and 30 June 1835.

He was transported to the Tauenzien regiment in Breslau and was torn from his homeland for a long time; his relatives complained and did not imagine that Koch's supposed misfortune would be the foundation of his happiness.

The commanding officer of his company treated him leniently and even permitted him to continue his bookbinding work after his hours of service. But another inclination—to music—began to animate the poorly educated youth. The rough life of his comrades was soon not enough for him. Equipped with a fine sense of hearing and, especially, a natural talent, even though he lacked a deeper knowledge of musical laws, he sought diversion and entertainment in music during his solitary hours. For lack of other means, it was, as mentioned above, the hitherto unexplored and poorly regarded instrument which he used for this purpose on his guard duty—the Jew's harp. His musical sense and the silence of the night, favorable to his experiments, permitted him gradually to discover a more consummate method of playing the instrument. He learned to produce sweet, flute-like tones on it by utilizing the echoing vibrations of the steel tongue in an ever more expedient manner and gradually eliminated the hard, twanging tones. Koch's talent would perhaps have remained unnoticed had it not been for a coincidence that occurred. An officer who was passing a guard post in Breslau one night suddenly heard sounds whose magical sweetness moved him strangely and urged him to investigate their origin more closely. Koch, at first afraid of punishment for an infraction of his duty, did not want to admit his discovery immediately, but the matter could not be concealed, and the officer, to whom the astounding artistic accomplishment seemed almost unbelievable, could not help informing the art-loving Prince von Hohenlohe Oehringen und Ingelfingen, then governor of Breslau, of the rare impression made by the unusual virtuoso whom he had in his garrison. Koch was ordered to go to the prince, in whose salon he was heard with admiration and approval. Through the prince, this remarkable new artistic talent came to the knowledge of the king of Prussia, Friedrich Wilhelm II, who, because of the exceptional nature of the matter, had Koch come to Berlin and perform before the assembled court. All the noble personalities expressed their keenest interest. Princess Friederike, later Duchess of York, was particularly moved by the beautiful impressions she received and, through her intercession, effected Koch's discharge from military service. Thus, encouraged by approbation and rewards, in 1791 he began those artistic tours through Germany which were to occupy most of his life. He exercised his universally recognized artistic talent in almost every major city of the kingdom, bringing a great deal of pleasure; and when his audience acted on him in a stimulating and inspiring manner, his artistic talent increased, but he

still retained an amiable modesty that was characteristic of him. Many
written accounts of his unpretentiousness, as well as the respectability
of his behavior, were found among the works left in his estate. Like a
traveling student, he wandered from place to place, quickly at home
everywhere and scarcely seen.

It seems that Koch led this life until 1824, after which, tired of his
nomadic existence and in possession of means of financial security, he
retired. In Breslau, where his musical career had begun, he lived for
several years quietly and unnoticed, until 1831 when the public an-
nouncements of his death awakened the memory of his charming performances in many who had known and admired him. Koch had a
number of imitators and there were also many who developed further
the branch of art which he had created. The Jew's harp, raised to the
status of a fine musical instrument, has found a great deal of attention
among amateurs, and the unquestionably poetic effect it produces in the
hands of a skilled player can certainly not be called a mere trifle, as some
people are wont to do. The merit of having made the beginning and
given the stimulus will always belong to our Koch.

On his numerous travels he came into contact with many outstanding
men and, as a result of a little easily forgivable vanity, he tried to obtain
their autograph comments in an album. In this way, an extremely interesting four-volume album developed, in which, along with a great deal
of chaff, there is much that is clever and characteristic to be found.
Although I was not closely acquainted with Koch, when I heard the
news of his death I recalled an enthusiastic remark of Jean Paul's about
Koch's Jew's harp that I had read somewhere. Further inquiry brought
me information about the existence of this album, which I was finally
able to purchase.

I would now like to present some of the generally interesting comments and aphorisms drawn from that book, where, by the way, I
obtained most of the above information on Koch's life. Schummel
[Breslauer Almanach] evidently used the same source.

1. The soul finds its Arcadia again in these tones; and, at the same
   time, in this Arcadia there is a twilight and a dawn which show us
   what has set and what will rise for us.

   May nothing set for you which does not rise again, fresher and
   brighter, in the east.

   Weimar, 25 April 1800   Jean Paul Fr. Richter

2. After almost thirty [sic] years, I am writing again in your albums. I
   heard you just today, on the birthday of our Goethe, whose pro-
   founder years are sanctified by the heart for the gentler musical art,

for the moon-rainbow of the ear, if one may so term it. May your life too, like one of your earthly tones, resound in such a far and beautiful distance. But when it dies, it will remain, like the tone, alive in another soul.

Bayreuth, 28 August 1819   Jean Paul Fr. Richter

(In what sort of light do these casually jotted remarks by Jean Paul about the poet-hero Goethe appear next to the seductive hostility of the ignorant regarding the man who is the pride of the nation? In what sort of light do they appear next to the assertions of the arrogant literary reformers to the effect that Goethe was the destroyer of German literature?)

In the book under discussion here, Goethe also expresses his interest in its owner's attainments—tersely, certainly, as was his nature, but in a sharply characteristic manner as well. Immediately after Jean Paul's lines, the following is found:

3. With thanks for the pleasure of an evening rich in tones.

Weimar, 15 March 1820   Goethe

Herder, too, whose formal recommendation of Koch's talent is also found, praises it in these words:

4. Harmonious spirits of the air resound in the ear, approaching from afar and departing in these fluting tones.

Weimar, 25 April 1800   J. G. Herder

Joining these three heroes in the colorful little book is a fourth, no less renowned: Klopstock, who, on 6 January 1796, inscribed some Horatian verses which added the praise that Koch had made the *trombe* (a French expression for the Jew's harp) a musical instrument. Several other individuals of lesser authority may be permitted to follow the most notable spirits of the nation, inasmuch as they wrote unfamiliar thoughts in the book.

5. The soul is raised above the finiteness of the lower spheres when the whispers of your gentle tones waft harmoniously around our ears.

Halle, 25 March 1804   A. H. Niemeyer

6. Your melody lifts the soul softly and gently, as the presentiment of immortality hovers about beautiful souls in solitary silence.

Halle, 25 March 1804   August Lafontaine

7.   The Jew's Harp

Deeply absorbed in holy, silent devotion,
I listen, enchanted, to the gentle, delicate sounds.
From far off clouds I hear, enraptured,
The sweet sigh floating in the melody;
I imagine that I hear the faint echoing
Of singing, transfigured angelic choirs.

Berlin, 25 February 1804   G. Starke

8.   To Koch

If someone wishes to hear spirits drifting
And souls traveling back and forth,
Let him build himself a marble hall
With vaulted roof and oval wall;
Let him seat his girl near himself
And clasp three of her fingers gently
And chastely, and call you
To come into his marble hall,
To extinguish the lights altogether,
To strike your magic steel:
Thus will he hear spirits drifting
And souls traveling back and forth.

Altenburg, 18 March 1800   Anton Wall

9. To help me out of my magic dreams,
   I declare you musician of the elves.

Stuttgart, 27 January 1820   Fr. Haug

Many interesting entries from people still living succeed those of the
spirits of the past. I do not feel justified, however, in presenting here
thoughts not specifically intended for the general public. But I cannot
deny myself the publication, here at the end, of the verses by the witty
Dr. Justinus Kerner and those of my friend and countryman, Carl von
Holtei. May their authors not hold it against me!

10. Who gave you this magic iron?
    Who consecrated your earthly mouth?
    Listen! Are those not the melodies of heaven?
    Man stands allied with spirits.
    Such tones are heard resounding
    By the dying man who softly says,

"My friends, do you hear the singing too?"
His friends, though, do not hear it.

Heilbronn, 29 January 1820   Dr. Justinus Kerner

11. In the wreath that Vienna bound for you,
    Let me twine a little flower too.
    Joyfully, I offer you my hand,
    Happy to find a countryman here.
    Travel on, surrounded by gentle tones,
    Travel on in good fortune,
    For in the kingdom of truth and beauty,
    Every place is home.

Vienna, September 1823   C. von Holtei

With this, let us take leave of the wandering musician and our consideration of his artistic achievements which, although unassuming, were filled with such poetic temperament and were so powerfully moving!

Eulenstein's Musical Career

KARL EULENSTEIN

EDITED BY FANNY ROODENFELS

Foreword

When a sketch of my father's life from the pen of Adolf Palm appeared two years ago in *Die Gartenlaube*, I was asked by many music lovers to publish something more detailed about the artistic life and work of my father, as well as a closer description of his Jew's harp.

The International Exhibition for Music and Theater in Vienna, where the instruments left by my father are displayed, provides the most advantageous opportunity to comply with this wish, and I present herewith to the public my father's autobiography. I have little to add thereto. Moderate as my father was in everything, he also avoided praising his own playing and his successes. The reviews of "Eulenstein's Jew's harp playing" which appeared during his time may now be permitted to speak for him, and I reproduce a few of them here below.

The Times, 5 August 1830

We had the opportunity to hear Mr. Eulenstein play the Jew's harp. This was certainly a musical rarity in that beautiful tones were combined with brilliant performance in such a manner that those who wished to judge the obvious capacity of such a worthless and insignificant instrument could scarcely imagine it. The tones produced by our artist are very similar to those of an aeolian harp, but are much softer and far more pleasant to the ear. He uses about twenty Jew's harps, which lie before him, plays upon two or four simultaneously and changes them during play with a speed which causes not the slightest interruption in the music. The extent of his scale is from the lowest C to the first E over the line and thus comprises four octaves and two notes. Each of his instruments has a fundamental tone with many incidental tones, so that he is able to play all sorts of music. Among others, Mr. Eulenstein performed the piece "Di tanti palpiti" by Rossini, to which our artist composed four variations. In this piece he

Dedicated to Her Highness Princess Pauline von Metternich. Stuttgart: Strecker and Moser, 1892.

effects the staccato, legato, and chromatic transitions with accuracy and a truly astounding facility.

The Examiner, no. 960

A few days ago, we were astonished at the playing of Mr. Eulenstein, the well-known Jew's harp virtuoso. For those who have only heard the instrument from a travelling Tyrolean, it would be extremely difficult to obtain an adequate idea of Mr. Eulenstein's playing. He is the only artist who has achieved great fame through his playing of the Jew's harp. It has also been his honor to play before royalty with great success in England and Paris.

The Times, 31 May 1833

Performances on the Jew's harp. Mr. Eulenstein, whose playing on this unpromising instrument caused such a great sensation during last year's concert season, is giving new proofs of his unique talent again this year in Hanover Square Rooms. By his handling of this hitherto disregarded instrument, Mr. Eulenstein has raised it to one of great beauty and significant rank. The high tones, if somewhat weak, are extraordinarily delicate and ingratiating, the lower ones are, on the other hand, strong and expressive. In his hands, the Jew's harp is able to summon forth the most beautiful sensations in us which good music may generally produce. In his concert of yesterday, Mr. Eulenstein offered us a rich selection of significant and elegant pieces, which were all marked by brilliant execution and real pathos. The famous Irish song, "Kathleen O'Moore," was among these and was performed masterfully with great taste in its inserted runs and trills. A Rondo à la Paganini, a piece whose rendering on the Jew's harp would be thought an impossibility, was performed by Mr. Eulenstein in such a manner as to gain him the warmest approval of the public. The brilliant runs, the staccato, and double tones, among others, were reproduced remarkably from Paganini's characteristic and thrilling effects, and with purity of execution. The whole offered an exquisite delight and we noted with pleasure what a numerous and select audience attended the performance by this extraordinary talent.

New Court Journal, 1 June 1833

After hearing the extraordinary performance of this gentleman, we must quickly withdraw our groundless judgment against his hitherto disdained instrument, the Jew's harp, in order to do justice to both him and ourselves. We are only expressing our full conviction if we assert that our ear has never been so pleased by the confluence of attractive melodies, that we have never been so astonished and enchanted at the same time. Our readers cannot imagine the "silver notes," the "sweet harmonies," the "swelling cadences" and the "dying" tones which Mr. Eulenstein produces on this simple instrument. We might have easily believed ourselves removed to fairyland if the stormy applause of the audience had not torn us from our dreams!

Literary Gazette

Our modest, talented and worthy friend and favorite, Mr. Eulenstein, arranged another proof of his superb Jew's harp playing for his admirers in London. We have frequently described the extraordinary effect which he produces on this simple instrument by tuning a number of them in a certain scale and changing them with uncommon speed during play, without at all interrupting the melody or impairing the brilliant performance. But since we last heard him, when he played before His Majesty, the late King George IV, Mr. Eulenstein has made great progress in his skill. By increasing the range of tones of his Jew's harps, he has lent their former sweetness more strength, and his performance is now extremely sensitive and delicate, possessing organ-like swellings united with the dying cadences of the aeolian harp. This splendid result gives the most distinct proof of his great inborn talent. It is unlikely that a successor will be found who will offer a performance in this manner. The magical tones will live and die with him.

"Upon Eulenstein's Playing the Jew's Harp at Night"
[This poem is presented in a slightly different form later in the text of the autobiography—TRANS.]

> Does what I'm hearing come from bees?
> No, they do not swarm at night.
> Now it sounds like ghostly choirs of
> Dainty sylphs, faint and shining;
> Louder now, like ringing harps,
> Gently moved by swaying breezes.
>
> And from these tones
> Clear, delicate forms arise,
> Stars and flowers I see floating,
> Wonderful, magical signs.
> Let light appear: sorcery will bind us
> To what we find.
>
> Ha! It is the familiar good spirit
> Who, with his iron, shows us
> The land of spirits
> Through supernatural means.
> But he is silent, and slowly
> We sink below again to earth.

Justinus Kerner

"To Eulenstein, Musician on the Jew's Harp"

If suddenly, in silent night,
Someone, half dreaming, half awake

Could hear the magic of your tones,
Listening, he would ask: "Have I already
Left the idle dust of earth,
Been greeted by pure angelic choirs?"
So it was when I sat and listened,
Almost forgetting to draw breath;
Amidst these wondrous sounds the rapture
Wished to burst out from my breast.
These tones are not of this world,
They are the sounds of gentle spirits
Which God entrusted for your consecration,
Harmonies from the tent of stars,
Sent to us mortals here—
A foretaste of the higher life.

Neuffer

When my father could no longer play the Jew's harp, as a result of losing his teeth, he set his hand to the guitar and brought a rare virtuosity to this instrument as well. All the pieces which he played in concerts were composed by himself, of if he played variations on one or another well-known theme, these were by him. From the description of his childhood, it is evident that he had a delicate constitution; he often fainted, which even occurred several times on the street. Through his tenacious energy and his force of will, he achieved, despite everything, an independent existence after twenty years of hard work, and he was able to return at the age of forty-five to his native city, Heilbronn am Neckar. Enigmatically, he spent less time on his all-consuming love of music than on collecting fossils, minerals, shells, and the like. He constructed a telescope whose lens he himself ground; he worked with a microscope, devoted himself to gardening and achieved a great deal here too. The inhabitants of Heilbronn liked to come out and see his rare plants by day and his telescope by night—or much more, to look at the moon through the telescope.

Young people who are left to their own resources can learn much from him. Above all, they can learn that it is possible to make something important out of a very small insignificant thing, even with the most limited means. Great perseverance, frugality, iron diligence, indefatigable zeal and especially faith in God triumphantly overcome all obstacles which arise in one's path. My father went as a poor, weakly youth into the world—provided with nothing but his Jew's harp, and he often describes movingly in the sketches of his life which follow how badly things frequently went for him. Nevertheless, he conquered with almost superhuman strength, given to him by his love of music, and did not rest until he had reached his goal.

It was only after the death of his faithful wife that he threw himself fully into music again, choosing the violin. In his eightieth year he composed over sixty pieces for violin, some of which have appeared through G. A. Zumsteeg's music publishing company in Stuttgart.

On his eighty-seventh birthday he played a Bach fugue on the violin before a small audience, but thereby made the sad discovery that his physical strength was no longer sufficient. For the first time in his life he complained about his age; otherwise he indignantly rejected everything that is a necessity for old people; he scorned every comfort which one usually permits oneself at this age, because he considered that he was not yet old enough for such things. On the last Christmas of this life, he was almost insulted when he was given a fur coat, and he said that he did not need to be coddled. When he was no longer able to perform music, however, he foresaw that he would soon have to die. Unfortunately, this presentiment was fulfilled several weeks later.

On the day of his death (8 January 1890), he asked to hear his favorite song which he had composed, "Die Sehnsucht" [Longing], and which his musical daughter-in-law, Olga (née Pischek) had arranged for piano on his last birthday. He sang his "last song" in a strong voice.

A few hours before his death, he suddenly sat up, opened his eyes wide and wanted to speak, but could no longer do so. He gripped my hand tightly, nodded to me with a happy smile and moved his mouth very strangely. Those who stood around his bed did not know what to make of this, but I understood: he believed that he was playing his beloved Jew's harp; he imitated mechanically the undertones, just as he used to do when playing the Jew's harp. His radiant, shining eyes, his joyful expression, so moved the people assembled there that all of them wept. He then closed his eyes, as though he had fallen asleep—but his soul had gone to a better world, full of harmony. I must add something else, although in our material world one does not speak of wonders without being mocked and ridiculed. As though heaven itself wished to attest that a great, noble spirit had entered the Elysian Fields, at the moment in which his coffin was lowered into the grave—it was just 5:00 in the afternoon—a meteor fell with a shining, greenish gleam. This miraculous sign, as the fall of a meteor during the day at a funeral while the coffin was being lowered must be viewed, was observed by the mourners and many other inhabitants of Cillis and the vicinity. For me, however, this rare phenomenon of nature had a very special significance. For it occurred not only at the moment when the coffin was being lowered, but also at the same instant that I had raised my eyes to heaven with the anxious question: Is there another meeting? Is he united with his already transfigured love? It was as though the heavens opened and this comforting reply was given to me: "Yes, there is another meeting, he is united with his love—souls live forever, even if the body turns to dust!"

So I close with the last words of love which I have dedicated to my unforgettable, dear father as an "obituary":

> So you too are separated from me,
> Your father's heart no longer beats,
> The most devoted left to me
> In my brimming sorrow!
>
> Henceforth I must bear alone
> My nameless, deep pain;
> Your mouth will no longer utter comfort
> And all abandoned now I stand.
>
> But what should I complain about?
> I know that you are now with God:
> The angels carried you
> Aloft where our homeland is.
>
> You are united with our loves,
> Rest peacefully now in your God;
> And I am only left with grief
> Which death alone can heal.
>
> On high you harmonize with the holy hosts
> A song of praise before God's throne,
> Full of melodies, wondrously clear,
> As you often did in life.

Fanny Roodenfels

Eulenstein's Musical Career

My musical career, which I intend to describe in this book, actually began at the age of twenty-two; but I experienced so much in my early youth which affected it that the reader will forgive me if I begin my little story with a description of my early years.

I was five years old when I lost my father. The little that he left was not sufficient to bring up my sister and myself, and my mother was thus obliged to return with the two children to her parents' home, where she was received joyfully. Two years later, however, my grandfather died and my mother was left helpless in the world. She received a thousand gulden as her inheritance. An uncle took my sister in and I remained with my mother who, though, because of her needy circumstances, could spend very little on my upbringing. My grandfather on my father's side was still alive, but was hard-hearted enough to forbid all three of us his house simply because he had quarreled with my father. All descriptions of our tragic situation were useless, and only as a result of the continued intercession of several friends did he finally consent to give my mother thirty gulden a year, but on condition that this amount, together with interest, would be deducted from our inheritance after his death, and also that none of us would enter his house. Thus did a rich man treat his poor grandson. Because he lived another twenty years, the sum later deducted from the inheritance was very large, due to interest. This was certainly hard, but it was a thousand times harder for me to have to pass by the home of a rich grandfather every day without being able even to set foot in his house or to sit in one of his many gardens. The thought was then awakened in the seven year old boy that I was to leave my native city (Heilbronn am Neckar).

The reader may well imagine that my mother was able to rent only a very small lodging on her small income; it consisted of a single room and was in the house of a tailor. Our food was very meagre and I often had only dry potatoes to eat for months at a time. Despite all these economies, the small income was by no means sufficient. The capital had to be encroached upon and my mother fearfully watched the approach of destitution. These privations did not make me at all unhappy, since I enjoyed great freedom in spite of our poverty. My mother was an extremely kind-hearted woman who loved me tenderly and, as she could not provide me with any amusements in her little dwelling, nor had any means to buy me books, she permitted me to remain in the streets after school. I made ample use of this opportunity and frequently played with other street urchins until nine o'clock in the evening. This had the inevitable detrimental consequences for me that from day to day I became more badly behaved; and if this way of life had continued much longer, I would now perhaps be a tailor or shoemaker in some small town of Württemberg. But something else happened.

When I was eight and a half years old, I was admitted to the gymnasium and, at the same time, to the Heilbronn Choir Institute, where I received free lessons in singing and violin playing. Already as a four year old child I had demonstrated a great weakness for music and as a street urchin I ran all over where there was music to be heard. My mother, however, took no notice of this, as she never imagined that I could make my fortune through music. The very first day of my entrance into the Institute brought about a great change in my life, for what my mother could never do by any means to keep me off the streets, the violin suddenly accomplished. My father had left a violin, but without a bow, so that my mother had packed it away years before. It was now brought out and a bow was bought for it. On the day when I had my first violin lesson, I also came into possession of my violin and now I was as though suddenly transformed. I spent much less time in the streets and devoted most of my free time to my violin, which from then on was my greatest treasure. My desire to learn was so great that when my mother sometimes had to chase me out of the room, I would run to the upper part of the house, even in winter, and continue to play until all my fingers were frozen.

When my mother realized this, and when she heard from my teacher that he had never had a student who made such great progress as I, she began to believe that I was a born musician and even conceived the hope that I would someday be able to support her through this talent. I also believe that she would then have yielded to my insistent request to dedicate myself completely to music if her uncle (the same one who had taken my sister in and without whose advice she would not do anything) had not protested, partly because, as the reader will learn later, he had an extraordinarily poor opinion of musicians and partly because he had decided that I would become a tailor.

This uncle was a simple, unpretentious man who, through his industry as a dyer, had earned a fortune. He thought of musicians as idlers and vagabonds, and although he often heard that I had a very special talent for music and that I was making unusually great progress on the violin, he remained by his decision that tailoring would suit me best. I did not let myself be deterred in any way, but continued to play my violin. Because I played so much, however, I needed many strings, and since my mother's small capital was constantly diminishing and she complained perpetually about her poverty, it cost me the greatest difficulty to ask her for money for a string. I therefore devised a means to help.

I convinced my mother that instead of my breakfast every morning (which consisted of a roll), she should give me a kreutzer, with which I would buy a roll for myself on the way to school. Now instead of buying a roll, I remained hungry until midday and in this way saved enough in six days to buy a string. When my mother found out about this, she was moved to tears and insisted that I should not acquire any more strings in that way. A small improvement in my lot also occurred at that time. It had become more and more widely known in what sad circumstances my mother existed, and a few wealthy women were found who helped her. They obtained cast-off clothing for me and sometimes a few notebooks and pencils. As I distinguished myself in gymnasium, I also received many prizes at the yearly examinations. These prizes, which today consist of worthless medals, were then useful objects: pen-knives, copy-books, etc., which came in handy for poor but diligent students and stimulated them to learn. This was true in my case as well. I also had the good fortune that richer boys sought my company and I was invited to visit their parents' houses. There, I had much bread and butter and apples, even delicacies; but more than this, the good treatment that I received in these homes made a deep impression on me.

Despite all these kindnesses, my mother's poverty grew daily and she now decided, although it was very difficult for her, to go into service. She became a nanny in a family which had formerly been much poorer than she herself, but which had become well-to-do. She had board and lodging, as well as a good salary; and as my uncle paid my tuition and provided all the required books, as well as assisting us in other ways, complete helplessness was at least deferred in this manner. I was boarded with the tailor in whose house we had lived. The cost of board for a year was fifty gulden and the reader may well imagine that at this price the tailor did not have much profit from me. But I was also very badly treated and not only did the master and his wife use me for every possible kind of work, such as carrying water, bringing wood into the kitchen, etc., but I also had to get beer for the journeymen and take their boots to the shoemaker; when I came from school, I had to take care of the small children and could only play my violin half as much as when I had lived with my mother. I also did not have my own bedroom, but was obliged to sleep in the same room as the tailor's apprentice.

This room was the only place where I could play my violin and because it was unheated, I suffered badly from the cold in winter. The worst, however, was that my rich young friends—at least some of them—began to avoid me, and this may well have been the main reason why my mother held out only a year at her employment. She left her service, took a small lodging, and now I was freed from my torments and could live with my mother again. The food that I had had at the tailor's was certainly better than what my mother could offer me, but in spite of that, I felt a thousand times happier than before and played the violin again to my heart's content.

My mother began to knit stockings for people and was decently paid for this work. I was again invited by the parents of my rich friends and, for some time, was very happy. I made great progress in both music and in Latin and Greek. As a student in the Choir Institute, I had to sing in church on Sundays, and in the afternoon I was usually invited to a musical family. But this happiness did not last very long. When my mother saw that, in spite of all her thrift, more and more of her small capital was disappearing, she thought again of going into service. She went to relatives in the country who had an inn and I was boarded this time with a factory foreman where I was a little better off than with the tailor. Here too, though, I had to play my violin in a cold room, but my mother returned and rented a third lodging. Who could have been happier than I when I was able to live with my mother once again!

Those who have the happiness to spend the whole of their childhood with their parents often do not know how to value this good fortune and it frequently happens that only after a separation of many years do they learn what a mother is. Many children would give less grief to their parents if they knew what mother-love is.

Now I could again play the violin in a warm room and my progress was also greater. When the time for my confirmation came, which was also the time when I had to choose a profession, I tried as hard as I could to convince my uncle that I was born to be something better than a tailor.

The time came and the idea was indeed given up, but my uncle fought against my following the profession of a musician, which I had naturally chosen. This was a great misfortune for me because, as my uncle paid my tuition, I had to obey him. I was sent to the chancery in Heilbronn, but I only lasted there six weeks. From the first day on, I continually tormented my poor mother to let me become a musician after all; only my uncle refused to be won over and when he heard that I absolutely did not want to remain a clerk, he insisted that I at least learn a trade. By coincidence, a bookbinder was looking for an apprentice and since I knew that this man was a great friend of music, I was completely satisfied when I was sent to him in order to learn. The term was four years with an apprenticeship fee of fifty gulden. My mother brought me there at ten in the morning and in a quarter of an hour I was already sitting at a table folding printed sheets into signatures. I worked until seven and then, after dinner, went to my mother for an hour, after which I was sent to bed at eight-thirty. Although it was completely dark, I was not allowed to take a light with me; instead, I was brought to the door of my bedroom and told, since it was a moonless night, that my bed stood in the corner on the left. I stumbled around for at least five minutes until I found the bed and when, after a great deal of trouble, I was finally able to lie down in it, I could not fall asleep for a long time, even though I was very tired because the bedclothes were so coarse and heavy that they lay on me like a hundred-pound weight and for some time I wondered whether I was really lying in a bed.

I passed the night with all kinds of thoughts, especially whether I would be able to play my violin somewhere here; finally I fell asleep.

When I awoke, I was amazed to see that I was in a storeroom in which hundreds of pieces of pasteboard and all sorts of paper stock were piled up. If I had to sleep in such a room now, I think I would suffocate; then, however, it did not bother me. I still knew that my master was a great amateur of music and that was more important than anything else. Despite this, I was forbidden to bring my violin into the house, but I could spend a few hours every evening after dinner with my mother, which was of great advantage to me, as I was able to continue with the violin. I also had Sunday afternoons free, which I spent either with my mother or with musical families.

I felt quite happy in my new situation and my employer also seemed to be very satisfied with me. I was therefore astounded when, after four weeks, he declared that he could not use me because I was too weak to be a bookbinder. This was a hard blow for me and an even harder one for my mother. I was as though destroyed and began to weep loudly. My mother wanted to expostulate with him, but he maintained his opinion that I was too weak for this trade. I was so overcome with pain that my mother had to drag me out by force. Because I cried all the way home, all the street urchins ran after us and the more my mother scolded them, the greater the crowd became. By the time we arrived home, we were surrounded by more than twenty urchins who, when we were already in the house, continued their laughter until the landlord finally drove them away.

Now I felt truly unhappy and my mother's circumstances weighed especially heavily on my heart. I did not dare to appear at my mother's uncle's, as I was afraid that he would again threaten me with tailoring. My only hope in this desperate situation was that I would be sent to study music, a wish that I repeated hourly to my mother. In order to give more strength to my entreaty, I played my violin continually from morning until night. When my mother declared, however, that she could not stand it any longer, I ran out of the room with my violin, up to the attic where I continued to play. This apparently bothered our land-lord's wife, since after a few hours the landlord himself came out and told my mother that unless that miserable scraping stopped, he would chase us out of the house. From then on, I never played outside our room and for a few days, in accordance with my mother's wishes, played only gentle pieces.

My mother was now advised from several quarters to send me to gymnasium for another year in order that I might learn more Greek and Latin, and then to apprentice me to a merchant.

I had neither the desire nor the talent for this plan and could also not understand what use Greek and Latin might be to a merchant; but I had to obey, because my uncle agreed and paid the tuition.

Thus I entered gymnasium for the second time, where I stayed only six months, though, instead of a year. It was the custom then in Heilbronn that one of the poorer gymnasium students be used as a funeral herald and I was chosen for this service. As I had, from child-hood, always been very shy and unassuming, and was extremely awk-ward before distinguished people, this duty was completely unsuitable for me. I felt this, certainly, but took it on anyway, since the gulden that I received for it was very useful to my mother. With the first funeral announcement that I had to make, I was obliged, coincidentally, to begin at a merchant's who happened to be in his office just then. I trembled from fear and stuttered out the memorized speech so clumsily that I almost remained stuck in the middle of it. In addition, I was wearing a frock-coat that had been given to me and which did not fit me at all. It was therefore no wonder that the merchant and his apprentices could barely restrain their laughter during my recitation. It did not go much better at the other visits I made and I can truly say that this was one of the most agonizing days of my life, on account of which I was also never again given the task of announcing a funeral. My mother very much regretted this, since she lost many gulden because of it.

After I had spent six months in gymnasium, my mother found an occasion to send me as an apprentice to a mercantile concern. The term of apprenticeship was five years, without tuition costs, and because my employer was generally known as a man of noble character, my mother considered herself fortunate to have provided so well for me, particularly because a kind of famine existed at that time in Germany and my mother and I had to live for several months on dry potatoes, which she received from a rich landowner as a gift.

From the first day, my employer treated me like his own child and I did everything I could to anticipate his wishes, and was also fortunate enough to earn his satisfaction. My attachment to this man was so great that I would have gone through fire for him. But since here on earth there is no complete joy, this happy period finally became bitter too. My employer's wife was a very domineering, ill-humored, and envious woman who hated nothing more than music, while my employer was a great amateur of music. No sooner did she hear that I had a special talent for music and that I played the violin well than she immediately sent for my mother and forbade me absolutely ever to bring a violin into the house. As I could only go out for a few hours every two weeks, I now had to neglect my violin playing completely, which was a difficult loss to me. I submitted to the interdict, however, to please my employer. To my good fortune, the oldest son of the family was very musical and he furthered my talent in secret by letting me have a horn for some time. This horn could certainly not replace my violin, but for me it was like a bad meal to a hungry man; better a horn, I thought, than no instrument at all.

I practiced at night before going to sleep and, as my bedroom was in a distant wing of the house, it was a long time before the evil woman found out. I was then prohibited from playing and although I had made very slight progress on the horn and was not much attached to this instrument, I was disturbed nonetheless and returned the instrument only with pain. My employer and the son who had lent me the horn ventured to take my part, but they made things worse that way. The horn had to be removed from the house and the evil woman tormented me from then on whenever she could. We had a bookkeeper at that time who had long seen with envious eyes how kindly I was treated by my employer. When this man now noticed that the woman of the house was angry with me, he incited her against me even more and sought to slander me to her by every means. This hurt me very much, as he was a drunkard and I, a moral young man who had nothing but my good name.

One day, a young peasant came to our office in order to make a small payment. I was there alone, took the money and gave him a receipt, after which he left quickly. Half an hour later, the bookkeeper discovered that a roll of ten gulden was missing, which he had placed on the desk a short time before in my presence. He was shameless enough to call me to account and declare that I must know where the roll went, since I had been in the office the whole time. I told him simply that I did not know anything about it, but that I suspected it had been taken by the peasant boy who had paid me the money. My employer, who had come in, believed me immediately and resolved to speak to the boy himself, as one could not take him to court. The boy was the son of a poor messenger-woman who had already enjoyed many kindnesses from my master; we knew that he had to return in three days and the questioning was put off until then. In the meantime, the bookkeeper forgot himself to the extent that he told my employer's wife that he believed I myself was the thief, since he considered me capable of such an act. The woman was careless enough to repeat this to my mother who, of course, told me. When I heard this, I first became completely enraged, but controlled myself immediately, because I knew that my employer considered me completely innocent. I did tell him, however, that the bookkeeper had cast suspicion on me to his, my employer's, wife, to which he replied that I should remain calm and he would see to it.

The young peasant came another morning at the usual time and was taken into the next room by my employer. He told the boy that three days before, a roll of money had been stolen at a time when no one else was in the office but he, and thus he must be the culprit. He also told him that if he confessed everything right away, he would be forgiven and presented with another ten gulden. At this, the boy confessed and later his mother came, wanting to return the money; my employer would not accept it back, but gave it to the poor woman as a gift.

One would have thought that the bookkeeper would have asked my pardon, but that did not happen; he simply denied that he had ever suspected me. I hoped that my employer would discharge the bookkeeper, but this did not occur, as he was a very capable manager and, despite his vice of drinking, a loyal servant. This event brought me a kronenthaler, given to me by my employer. This man was now even kinder to me than before, which further embittered the bookkeeper against me. The situation could have come to a bad end if good Providence had not suddenly sent me aid.

As the violin was once the cause of my not becoming a course street urchin, so now it was the Jew's harp which rescued me from my desperate circumstances.

We sold Jew's harps in our shop too. It was about this time that the famous poet Justinus Kerner from Weinsberg came to our shop to buy a few Jew's harps. I had already heard that a certain Koch gave recitals on the Jew's harp, but I had never heard anyone play who could perform anything special on this instrument, so I had never had the idea of playing it myself. While trying out the Jew's harps, Dr. Kerner played only a few notes, but these were so beautiful and made such an impression on me that I immediately decided to devote myself to this instrument. The same day, I bought several Jew's harps and used my first free moments to try and play them—without imagining that I would one day make my fortune with this little instrument.

When I went to bed that evening, I played from ten until two in the morning, and when I awoke at five, both Jew's harps lay beside me and had even scratched my face while I was asleep. I played for another hour in bed and had the inexpressible pleasure of being able to play a little piece after just one night. It was a waltz that I had composed myself that night and which I afterward played in all my recitals under the title "Trompetenwalzer," although naturally improved.

Who could have been happier than I was now! Despite everything, I had an instrument that I could play undisturbed and unheard. I had lacked something of the sort for so long and now I could pursue music regardless of the bookkeeper and my employer's wife. A Jew's harp cost only two kreuzer, too, and there were no strings to buy! I utilized every hour, every minute, to practice—whether in the shop, in the office, in the cellar, in the woodshed, in the attic—wherever I was alone. When I went to bed on the second evening, I tuned my Jew's harp somewhat lower by fixing a piece of wax or sealing wax on the end of the tongue. This had the effect of not only improving its tone, because the vibrations became slower, but it also had the advantage that the Jew's harp no longer scratched my face.

The second night, I already composed my second piece—a march. I played this march, too, later in my recitals, as I always retained a certain attachment to these two pieces. For a whole year I played for three or four hours every night and an hour and a half during the day, always in secret. My employer finally learned about it by accident and he invited a few friends in to hear me play. It was decided that I would play in the dark, in order to see whether the gentlemen would guess what instrument it was.

Aside from Dr. Justinus Kerner, who had heard me once, and my employer, no one knew or could guess; when the light was turned on, half a dozen Jew's harps lay on the table. Everyone was amazed that I could produce such varied tones on such an insignificant instrument, and after I had played a few more pieces, all of them said that they had never heard anything like it. Only one thing was unpleasant: when playing certain tones, I made terrible grimaces and contorted my mouth in a horrible way, which had a disturbing effect on my playing. It took almost a year until I was able to correct this fault by sometimes playing in front of a mirror. I should mention that neither the bookkeeper nor my employer's wife took part in the company described above and that neither of them ever heard my Jew's harps.

When I visited the poet Justinus Kerner several weeks later, he presented me with the following poem that he had written; I insert it here because it was the first ever written about my playing on the Jew's harp:

> Does what I'm hearing come from bees?
> No, they do not swarm at night.
> Now it sounds like ghostly choirs,
> Gentle sylphs, clear and soft,
> Now like little bells that ghostly dwarfs
> Are ringing in the mountains.
>
> And from these tones
> Clear, gentle forms arise—
> Stars—suns I saw floating,
> Wondrous magical signs;
> Let light appear: sorcery will bind us
> To what we find.
>
> Ha! it is the familiar good spirit
> Who, with his iron, shows us
> The land of spirits
> Through supernatural means.
> But he is silent, and slowly
> We sink below again to earth.

This poem (cf. also "Foreword") made such an impression on me that I decided on the way home to Heilbronn to develop myself into a virtuoso on the Jew's harp in the hope of later giving recitals on this instrument.

It happened that just around this time the Jew's harp virtuoso Koch came to Heilbronn in order to give a recital there. I received a free ticket from Dr. Kerner and was naturally exceedingly excited about this recital; my craving for it was so great that on the day of the recital I could neither eat nor drink.

The recital was quite well attended and I stood, solitary and alone, in a corner of the hall behind an oven. The playing had a powerful effect on me and when I came home, I immediately began to play—and played almost the whole night long. I had brought back the program and resolved not to rest until I could play all the pieces noted on it. This was accomplished in six weeks, although I could not perform the pieces with the extraordinary fluency of Herr Koch. Nonetheless, the hope was reawakened in me to earn my bread as a virtuoso on the Jew's harp. It was also then that I conceived the idea of playing on more than two Jew's harps at the same time. I tuned several Jew's harps in various keys, placed them on a table and changed them during my playing so that while I was playing on one Jew's harp, I quickly put the other on the table and, like a flash, brought a third to my mouth; thus, I could now pass from one key to another. As I practiced mostly in bed at night, it was not possible to make great progress in this new manner of playing, which had to be reserved for a later time.

I was now eighteen years old and had to endure another eleven months of my apprenticeship. After this period, I wanted to carry out my plan. Because I had no means, however, and because my uncle would not spend any money for me to attempt an artistic tour with the Jew's harp, besides the fact that my clothes were not good enough to appear in decently as a virtuoso, I was obliged at least to postpone my project.

I now recalled that I had a relative in Lüneburg who was a confectioner and whose son was a friend of mine. I wrote to him to inquire whether he could find a position for me in Lüneburg and received the reply that although he did not know of any position, he would take me on in his business, if I wanted to learn the confectionery trade, for four years without apprenticeship tuition. This was a sad prospect for me and my plans, but my uncle considered that it would be the best thing I could do and that my mercantile knowledge would be very useful later in a confectioner's shop. He also offered to pay for my fare and, in my desperate situation, nothing remained but for me to yield to my uncle.

I started off on the 11th of October 1821, after a difficult parting from my mother and sister, and arrived at my destination on the 29th at four in the afternoon. As I had made the whole journey on foot, I was very tired and exhausted, and a couple of days' rest would have done me a great deal of good. This was not allowed me, however, and I had to be at work in the bakery the next morning at six. Because it was before Christmas, when the confectioners have very much to do, I was made to work from six until eleven at night and quite often even until midnight or one. As an apprentice, I had to do the heaviest and most menial work, such as grating almonds, and since all the work took place in a hot bakery, the reader may well imagine how tired and sleepy I was at night after work. Nevertheless, I practiced my Jew's harp for several hours more when all had gone to sleep—not in bed, as before, but in the hot bakery, so that there were many nights when I slept no more than three hours. My longing to become a virtuoso on the Jew's harp was so great that all my efforts and work seemed a trifle if only I could play at length on my Jew's harp. As my employer was a great music lover, I had the immediate advantage that he did not forbid me my nightly hours of practice. These finally had to be stopped in any case, since my strength was being drained by these terrible exertions, and after a while I was able only to play in bed, where I would usually fall asleep after half an hour. When Christmas was over and business slackened, we had to work just until seven in the evening and I was now very happy indeed that I could devote the whole evening to my Jew's harp. In this, however, I had very much deceived myself. My employer soon saw that he could use me for all sorts of things and, as he had an inn and billiard parlor near his confectioner's shop, he conceived the idea of using me for that as well. I had to become the billiard marker, in which capacity I took turns with the son of the house. Fortunately, not much was played, but nonetheless I had to throw off my apron quickly several times a day in order to go into the billiard room. Unfortunately, I also had to mark often in the evening and wait on customers in the inn, so that I had few completely free evenings. In spite of this, I made great progress on the Jew's harp, as I was requested by the customers every evening to play something for them. This was very useful for me and also helped me to overcome, at least a little, my great shyness.

My employer also profited, since my Jew's harp brought many new customers to his inn. One of these customers lent me a violin and I was able to play that instrument for a while on Sundays; my employer organized occasional quartet evenings on which I played first violin. Precisely because of this, I continually thought still of becoming a musician, to which career the Jew's harp would open the way. The four-year apprenticeship contract, however, hindered me. Because it seemed almost impossible for me to hold out for so long, after much hesitation I wrote to my uncle that instead of learning the confectionery trade in the bakery, I was obliged to spend half my time in the billiard parlor and in the inn, and that I could not possibly endure this for four years.

My uncle was generous enough to write immediately to my employer and offer him one hundred gulden if he would shorten my apprenticeship to two years. My employer consented to this, took the hundred gulden, but still made me work in the inn as before, so that I learned little or nothing of confectionery.

Thus, another year passed, during which time my employer had a theater built behind our house at his own cost. Actors came to our house every day now, as well as to the inn, and I gradually became acquainted with the musical segment of this society. Some of them made a great fuss over my Jew's harp and declared that I had been born to be something better than a confectioner. This worked very much to my disadvantage, but what threatened to lead me away from the confectioner's altogether was the following coincidence. At that time a virtuoso named Kunert came to Lüneburg to give a recital on the Jew's harp. Because the people of Lüneburg already had an idea through me of what could be performed on this instrument, he had a large audience. Naturally, I was also there and was even more excited this time than I had once been in Heilbronn. I found that his playing was much better than mine. He did not have the brilliant staccato which I already possessed then, but in every other respect he was by far superior to me. Among other things, he played variations on the song, "Mich fliehen alle Freuden" [All Joys Flee from Me]. As this pleased me particularly, I decided to learn it the same night and, for that purpose, sat in the bakery from ten until three in the morning. In those five hours I learned the song and two variations, which I myself composed, and I played this piece the next evening for a few amateurs of music who said that they could find no difference between my performance of it and that of Kunert. This flattered me tremendously and stimulated me anew to perfect myself further. I continued to pursue my nightly practice with the greatest zeal and my progress was so great that within two months my patrons declared that I played just as well as Kunert and that I could, like him, give recitals.

In this, however, they were very much mistaken, for Herr Kunert was not only a great Jew's harp player, but was altogether a fine musician and possessed all the qualities necessary to a traveling virtuoso, while in my case the opposite was true. I felt all this keenly, but still could not rid myself of the thought that I would eventually attain to this career.

My apprenticeship was now coming to an end, and I racked my brain day and night about what I should do. I had not learned very much at the confectioner's and I had little courage for an artistic tour, since I lacked both money and experience. In these sad circumstances, I decided to ask my employer to permit me to give a recital in his theater. But because I lacked the courage to speak to him, I resolved to address him in writing. I wrote to him that all my friends and patrons were of the opinion that I should at least make an attempt with the Jew's harp, and that in Lüneburg he would be assured of a full house; I begged him urgently to permit me this.

I was astounded the next morning when he replied briefly to me verbally that he could not advise such a plan and that he considered it his duty to communicate my intentions to my uncle in Heilbronn.

This was most unexpected and caused me much anxiety, as he had sent my letter directly to Heilbronn. After eight days I received the following letter from my uncle:

Dear Karl,

Your own healthy reason can tell you how disquieting I found the letter of yours which Herr K. sent me. You know that I employed means to shorten your apprenticeship in order to facilitate your career, and now you want to choose a new occupation which does not deserve to be called an occupation, for no trade is less remunerative and less useful to man than this one, if it is not studied fundamentally in order to become a real musician, for which, however, great expenditures of money and time are required. Or do you want to be simply a violinist who plays at country fairs? You will never be a true musician who plays the piano, knows the thorough-bass, and plays all wind instruments. Don't you know the saying, "a rolling stone gathers no moss"? Someone who takes up a second and then a third trade becomes a good-for-nothing or a beggar. If you want to be an accomplished journeyman-musician, you must become acquainted with every instrument. Or do you perhaps want to become a virtuoso on one instrument? How is that possible? Exertions of every kind are required for it, and where are the wealthy musicians and virtuosi who are in a position to support a mother? I could enumerate dozens of musicians who have breathed their last in misery and poverty, hunger and sorrow. And you want to give up a trade paved with gold to build castles in the air? Musicians, virtuosi, and actors are all subject to chance and mostly have a tragic end. I ask you therefore to shun the delusive illusion which your imagination has painted and remain at the trade you have learned. Your music does not make you unhappy, but also does not earn you any money—only future conversation and admittance to musical circles, which you can find as a baker too. Listen to me and your sensible friends, of whom I have heard, who disapprove of and criticize your plans. Trust in God, pray, learn, and work diligently, and some day you will succeed. This is your loving uncle's true opinion.

J.C.K.

This letter was a hard blow for me, as I felt that in fact my uncle was right. I could do nothing else but obey him and give up all thoughts of concerts, at least for the time being.

I made a new contract with my employer and agreed to remain another six months with him as a baker's helper in return for a promise of good wages after the expiration of my apprenticeship. If he had let me work exclusively as an assistant in the bakery, perhaps I might actually have become an efficient journeyman baker eventually, but he found me too suitable for the shop and the inn to be able to dispense with me there. Because the clients asked about me every day, it soon went so far that I was assisting in the inn as much as before. The only difference was that I was now able to go out more in the evening and had more free time on Sunday afternoon. I utilized this time partly to visit families with whom I was friendly and partly to increase still further my proficiency in playing the Jew's harp.

When the time approached for me to leave my position, the thought awoke in me again that I should give a farewell concert. I first shared this idea with those clients of the inn who were my particular patrons. They supported my request to my employer who, after some reluctance, consented to my giving a concert in his theater. This took place very soon. But as it was the first time that I appeared in public, although I had prepared myself thoroughly, I did not play as well as usual because I was indescribably nervous, which affected the calm breathing so necessary in playing the Jew's harp. Nevertheless, I was warmly applauded after each of my pieces and everyone told me that I would make my fortune with such a talent.

This praise, together with receipts of 65 thalers, and the notion of an artistic tour again haunted my mind. As the reader will learn later, I was to repent it dearly.

After much reflection, I decided to start off on an artistic tour and if this should prove unsuccessful, I would look for work as a baker.

I set out on 1 June 1824, after a difficult farewell, together with a young friend of mine from Lüneburg. I was on foot, as I had come; the only difference was that I had arrived in Lüneberg without any money and now had 70 thalers.

As I had earned most of this money from a single concert, I could see nothing wrong in at least making a provisional attempt with the Jew's harp. My companion was a young button-maker whom I still feel sorry for to this day because he had to listen to my enthusiastic talk about art and artists constantly, in compensation for which I frequently played attractive pieces for him on the Jew's harp. At first he listened patiently, but when it became too much for him, he began to speak about his sister because he knew that I preferred above all to talk about her.

On the second day, we arrived in Celle, a little town in Hannover. I wanted to make my first attempt to give a concert here. I had a letter of recommendation to a Dr. Seybold, who organized private gatherings in his home where I could be heard and where my playing would be admired.

I ran around for two days, but as I lacked the necessary experience and the courage, I was unable to arrange a concert and was obliged to leave without having achieved my object. It was lucky for me that I had a companion who was very thrifty and that I did not need much money. Wherever we spent the night, if I did not give a concert there, I said that I was a baker, as I could travel much more cheaply in that capacity. Only in those towns where I wished to concertize did I call myself a musician, in which capacity I had to pay more, since I was obliged to stay in a better hotel.

The next place where I wanted to give a concert was Braunschweig, but it went no better there than in Celle, and after two days of useless running around I had to leave without performing. It went the same way in Göttingen, Kassel, and Frankfurt. My playing was admired everywhere, but I was nowhere able to give a concert.

I had now decided that I did not possess enough experience for this profession and was thinking of looking around for a place as a baker when I received a letter from my uncle with the news that my grandfather had died and saying that if I had not yet found a job as a baker, I should come to Heilbronn in order to attend to my inheritance myself.

I accompanied my friend to Mannheim, where he found work, and continued my journey alone on foot. On 1 July 1824 I arrived in Heilbronn and for the first time enjoyed the happiness of reunion.

I had thus made a journey of one hundred and forty hours without succeeding in giving a single concert; it was only fortunate that due to my extremely simple mode of life and my great thrift, I had only needed a little money. I now still had eleven ducats, which was a decent amount for my circumstances at that time. I was cured for a while of my craving for concerts, but my desire to devote myself completely to music remained unweakened in me. I had conquered the passion, but it required only a small impetus to awaken it again.

My next plan was to await my inheritance and then go to Stuttgart in order to look for work in a bakery. As the division of the inheritance was delayed, I wanted to try and give a few little concerts in the small towns of Württemberg. My uncle protested that this would be dangerous for me because a single good concert would divert me from my main profession. I told him, however, that this would be simply a little excursion, and some of his friends persuaded him that it would perhaps be better for me to give a few concerts and burn my fingers well. He finally acquiesced and I traveled by way of Weinsberg, where I received some letters of recommendation from my friend and patron Dr. Kerner, and then to Oehringen. There, I gave a small concert and then went to Friedrichsruche, the country seat of the Prince von Oehringen. The prince was on a journey, but because I had brought such good letters of recommendation, the princess consented to hear me play. An appointment was made for me at eleven in the morning and, as I had never played before the nobility, I became so nervous that I was unable to eat the whole day. The hour finally arrived when I was admitted and as I came into the drawing room, I dropped my hat out of nervousness, which increased my embarrassment even further. With many bows, I came to the table on which my Jew's harps were already arranged, and my nervousness was so great that my playing came off miserably; a few Jew's harps even fell out of my hand.

My compliments as I was leaving also came off badly, although I had practiced them in front of a mirror for almost a quarter of an hour.

I received four kronenthalers and the assurance that my playing had greatly pleased the princess, who was sorry that the prince was away. I was now very happy and in the evening was even regaled with a supper which tasted marvelous to me, as I had eaten nothing all day. The next morning I started off quite early on my journey to Hall, pleased with my earnings and proud of having played before a princess.

An hour's distance from Hall, I was caught in a frightful storm which was accompanied by such pouring rain that standing under a large tree was useless and not only my clothes, but also my knapsack and everything inside of it were soaked through; my shoes and stockings were covered with mud to the knees. In this wretched state I arrived at Hall in the evening. The innkeeper thought at first that I was a tramp, but when I told him that I was a musician he seemed to look at me with more sympathy and asked whether my effects and my instruments were being sent on after me or whether I was perhaps a singer. Upon my replying that neither the one nor the other was the case, his face fell. In order to end his doubts, I showed him my letters of recommendation, at which he immediately had me shown to a single room.

As it was not possible to dry my clothes quickly enough, I went straight to bed and fell asleep in no time.

The next day, after I had submitted my letters, I was advised to organize a subscription concert and to present the tickets myself to the notables of the town. I declared this to be too great a humiliation, but was told that it was the custom in Hall and that otherwise I would have too small an audience. I was obliged to accommodate myself to the situation accordingly, but on my first visit they said that they could not quite understand how it was possible to give a concert on the Jew's harp. But the first six signatures were very opportune for me, because these were the first families of the place, so in each house I played a piece for the family, whereupon the signature quickly followed.

I had never experienced this method of collecting subscribers, which could only succeed with Jew's harps, as it was very easy to have a couple of instruments in one's pocket. Soon, however, I had my fill of it and I sent a man around who collected a few more signatures for me. Despite all these preparations, only fifty people came. I therefore paid my bill that same evening and the next morning started my return journey on foot.

It was twelve hours to Heilbronn; I covered this distance in one day and arrived in Heilbronn late in the evening, again with the intention of returning to the baker's trade. I was prepared for reproaches from my uncle, but to my great amazement he did not say anything this time. The reason, as I later found out, was that in my absence Dr. Kerner had spoken with him in order to make him understand that it was not wise to suppress a genius. But the four kronenthalers that I brought back had a greater effect than advice, as well as convincing him of my thrift. So it came about that he gave his consent to my return to baking, but first to make a final attempt at earning something with my Jew's harp. One day before I was to set out on my journey, an event suddenly occurred which, without the help of Providence, could have brought me great misfortune.

I used to wear around my body, day and night, a linen band in which were sewn the gold pieces that I had earned from my concert in Lüneburg. There were still sixteen ducats in this band. The evening before my planned departure, I went swimming and, for the first time, took off the band so that the money would not become wet. When I got dressed, I left the band lying there without noticing it—a thing I cannot understand to this day. Even more incomprehensible is the fact that I still did not notice that the belt was missing when I went to sleep. It was only when I awoke in the morning that I suddenly realized it was missing. I flew out of bed like an arrow, fell on my knees, dressed in a moment and ran out so quickly that my mother was afraid I had gone mad. In total despair and completely out of breath, I arrived at the place where I had to have left the band, but it was gone! The reader may excuse me from describing the pain I felt at that moment; aside from the great loss which shattered all my plans and robbed me of all my hopes, it was the thought of my poor mother which distressed me horribly.

After I had stared fixedly at a point for a minute, I pulled myself together again and was about to return home when a young friend came to the place to bathe. In the greatest haste, I told him of my misfortune and then wanted to go home in order to console my mother. I had not gone twenty paces, however, when my young friend called me back and beckoned to me. Reluctantly, I went back and he pointed at an old willow tree in which, he said, there seemed to be hanging something which looked like a belt. I climbed the tree as quickly as a cat and when I came to the branch, I suddenly saw that it was my belt and that the ducats were still in it. I learned only the next day that some young people who had been bathing after me had found the belt and thought that the ducats were pieces of lead. One of the boys tied the belt around his body, declaring that it was a remedy for cramps. The boys later threw the belt back and forth in the water until finally one of them threw it toward land, where it remained hanging on the willow tree.

My joy was now as great as my sorrow had been before. I threw the belt down and followed it in one jump. I thanked my young friend and ran home just as quickly as I had come. The half hour that I had been away had seemed an eternity to my mother, and who could have been happier than we two when I was home again! I immediately gave the money to my mother for safekeeping and never again wore a belt around my body. It is remarkable that I first began to weep when I came to my mother with the money.

My new artistic tour was postponed for a few days and, as I heard that the Prince von Oehringen had returned and was sorry that he had not been at home when I played there, I decided to go once more to Friedrichsruhe.

It was three in the afternoon when I arrived there and as soon as the prince heard of my presence, he asked that I be told that he wished to hear me in the open. I took my Jew's harp case under my arm and walked with great embarrassment to the arbor in which the prince was sitting. My innate shyness manifested itself here again. As I approached the arbor, I searched with my eyes for the prince and believed that I had found him in a man who was wearing a long beard. I made my compliments to him, but was not a little surprised when he did not greet me at all. The prince immediately noticed my error and spoke to me. My embarrassment was now so great that I could scarcely reply, and I was glad when he requested me to play. Contrary to my expectation, it went well this time: the prince was extremely pleased when he dismissed me and he rewarded me well. I went quickly to Weinsberg the same day and from there traveled to Heilbronn, where I arrived at ten at night.

The next day I went to my uncle, who was delighted indeed with my rapid earnings and the honor with which I had met. On this trip I had visited Dr. Kerner's brother-in-law, Bailiff E., in Oehringen; he had told me that he was going to Karlsruhe in a few days in his own carriage and had offered me a free place in it. I had accepted with pleasure and my uncle was also not opposed; he even consented to my venturing to give a concert in the meantime in my native city. This was quickly arranged, but only fifty people came, so that after paying my costs only a little money remained. My playing was so admired, though, that everyone who met me the next day encouraged me to give a second concert. This again was rapidly organized and after what people had told me, I was counting on an audience of 150. Only twenty-five came, however; the others had free tickets. Vexed and ashamed at the poor attendance in my native city, I went again to my patron in Weinsberg for consolation and learned that the Bailiff of Oehringen was traveling to Karlsruhe the next day and would call for me in Heilbronn. The following morning at nine the coach was standing in front of the house, which gave my uncle great pleasure. I took 40 guilders with me for traveling expenses and began this artistic tour with great hopes.

However, just as a stone, when it is thrown, does not always hit the mark at which it is aimed, so too was I disappointed in my hopes this time; everything turned out differently from what I had imagined. The whole way to Heidelberg nothing else was spoken of but my concerts, and when we came to that city we met Prince August von Oehringen, who had enjoyed my Jew's harp playing so much. In Heidelberg too, I met a Count Lean, whose resemblance to the Emperor Napoleon was as great as one egg to another. The count invited me to visit him, and it was thus that I received my first encouragement to go to Paris. From that day on, I thought a great deal about Paris—and it was always the idea of going there to make my fortune. We traveled to Karlsruhe and spoke the whole way only about Paris. When we arrived in Karlsruhe, Prince August was already there, and on our first day we accompanied the prince and viewed the sights. During this time, I occasionally played my Jew's harp for the prince, and when he expressed his desire to play the Jew's harp too, I presented him with a small case of five or six tuned Jew's harps.

After the prince and the bailiff had departed, I began immediately to pay visits in order to arrange a concert, but was obliged to run around a tremendous amount until I was able to accomplish this.

The people who helped me were: Herr Braun, a bookseller; Herr Burghardt, a cashier; and Captain Fischer, adjutant to the Margrave Wilhelm.

According to my accounting, I had to sell at least seventy tickets to cover the costs of my trip and other expenses. Only thirty people came, however, so that I was obliged to lose my own money, which was very painful for me. The only thing that still consoled me was that I had the honor to play before the Margravine Frederike, the future queen of Sweden. The grand duke was in Baden, where I did not dare to go, as there were so many famous artists there and I still did not have any renown. Both in my concert and before the margravine, I met with great approval, and now practiced the high art of living on prestige. My lunch often consisted of nothing but bread and cheese and a glass of beer; in the evening I went to bed hungry and pretended in the hotel that I had been invited out.

I now wanted to go to Pforzheim, but after two hours, one of my shoes began hurting me so much that I could no longer walk. As I did not have any extra money with which to ride, and also did not wish to remain behind, I decided to go barefoot and put my shoes on again just in front of the gates of Pforzheim. It was even worse for me in this city. On the evening of my arrival I played before a private gathering, and the next morning I went to the bailiff to obtain permission to give a concert. When I had asked to be announced, he came to the door violently, whereupon I wanted modestly to make my humble request. Without listening to me, he shouted, "Can't be!" and slammed the door in my face. I stood there like a poor wretch, embarrassed almost to death in front of the maid-servant who had heard everything. Furious, I returned to my hotel and within the hour I was outside the gates of the city.

Partly because of my bad foot and partly to spare my stockings, I again went barefoot, but after an hour I was caught in a downpour like the one near Hall. I had to put on my shoes and stockings once more and limped to Bretten. The next morning I went barefoot to Bruchsal where, with the help of Auditor Sommer, I arranged a concert which was rather well attended. From there I went via Heidelberg to Darmstadt, where Herr Landhas, the painter, gave me an extremely friendly reception. A concert was arranged, but the reader may well imagine my grief when, instead of the hundred people I was expecting, only twenty-five came and, after deducting my costs, I realized only 1 guilder, 6 kreuzer.

I was now seized with such sorrow that I wept half the night through and was on my way the next morning at five. Of the 40 guilders that I had taken with me, only 5 guilders remained. With these I made the return journey to Heilbronn in four days on foot. I had quite enough time during this trip to reflect on my cruel fate. It was indeed hard that a journey on which I placed all my hopes and during which I had imposed upon myself every possible privation should have such a sorry end. In addition, there was the disgrace of again being scolded as a vagabond by my uncle, who had already begun to have a better opinion of my talent. I was, in fact, in the most wretched state and my only hope now lay in my inheritance; but this too turned out extremely badly. Instead of the many thousands of gulden which we had expected, my sister and I together inherited 1,800 guilders. After this small fortune had been put out at interest for my mother's benefit, I decided to go to Stuttgart and look for work in a bakery there.

A vast flood, which placed the whole district under water, held me back for eight days, during which time I had sufficient opportunity to reflect on my past fate. Instead of that, however, I thought constantly about the future, and even now when I might have been convinced that I lacked all the qualities of a traveling virtuoso, even now I could not get the Paris castle in the air out of my head, and I nourished the silent hope that if I were not successful in going to Paris as a virtuoso, perhaps I could go there later as a baker.

To return again to my luckless journey, I had no idea then that those great hardships and privations also had their good side: if my concerts had yielded large receipts right from the beginning and if everything had gone according to my desires, in all probability I would have become overconfident and would not have been able to bear greater misfortune later; because things had gone so badly for me at the beginning, I was protected from pride and overconfidence.

As a result of unpleasant consequences, I learned the necessity of thrift, which is, unfortunately, found among so few artists because they overvalue their talent, whereby they are frequently induced to greater expenditures. If some budding young artist should read these lines, I advise him not to be seduced by high praise, whether spoken or written in newspapers, but always to remain modest. Excessive modesty, however, is not suitable everywhere and there are occasions when it is necessary to put it aside, e.g., at a restaurant table or especially in a hotel; but in general it may be stated that a budding young artist or private tutor will go farther with modesty than with arrogance. I can also not help saying here that young artists may be assured that nothing harms them more than always speaking detrimentally about their colleagues. This is especially applicable to young teachers. I too was flattered in every possible way on the hapless artistic tours described above; but my purse showed me only too clearly how much I could believe this high praise—just as the state of the stock market is often a much more reliable barometer of political events than all the newspaper articles.

After this brief digression, which I trust the reader will excuse, I return once again to my story. On 4 November 1824, I traveled to Stuttgart, where a relative had offered me free board and lodging. Although I had brought several letters of recommendation from Dr. Kerner, I did not make use of them at first, but wanted to look for work in a bakery before anything else, as I had promised my uncle. I went with a heavy heart from one baker to another, but everywhere in vain. I continued this melancholy business for two days and only when all hope of finding work had disappeared, I submitted my letters of recommendation, which were all addressed to the poets of Stuttgart. These people now received me quite differently from the bakers and two days later I played at a gathering in the house of the poet Gustav Schwab. In attendance at this gathering were Ludwig Uhland, Hauff, and various music lovers, and I happened to play much better than usual that evening, so that I received unusual acclaim. The next day I played at a gathering in Cannstatt, where I received 3 kronenthaler. Here I met Baron von Gemmingen of Bonfeld who, when I visited him the following day, gave me a letter of recommendation to his son, who was then chamberlain to the widowed queen in Ludwigsburg. I went to Ludwigsburg that same day and after Herr von Gemmingen had read his father's letter, he said that he believed he would be doing me the greatest service if he told me the truth: namely, that the queen hated music and that I had little chance of being admitted, but that he would do his best.

As I had come from Stuttgart on foot and was hungry and thirsty, I went to a hotel in order to refresh myself. I heard there that a group of gentlemen and ladies from the court were just then in the sitting room of the hotel to attend a concert rehearsal. When they learned that I was there, they expressed the desire to hear my Jew's harp. My playing must have pleased them very much, because two hours later I received word from Herr von Gemmingen that the queen wished to hear me.

I learned afterward that a group of gentlemen and ladies had joined at table to convince the queen to listen to my Jew's harp. I received the invitation on a Saturday and I was to play on Monday evening. The reader cannot possibly imagine how nervous I was for two days: the impending fulfillment of a long-cherished desire filled me with anxiety. I could not stand being in my room and ran around outside the whole day. Because things had gone so badly for me until now and I was more used to poverty and misfortune, the very high honor that had befallen me was bound to increase my ambition and eagerness to the greatest degree, so it was thus no wonder that during these two days I made every possible plan, which included playing at the English and Russian courts.

Monday came and I was to appear before the queen at eight that evening. I already began to dress by four and when I was finished, I ran up and down the room for several hours practicing the bows and compliments which I thought to make before the queen. I then practiced my pieces on the Jew's harp for an hour and finally, in the greatest anxiety, I went to the palace, where I was obliged to wait for an hour in the antechamber.

When I entered the hall, I began at the door to make deep bows which the queen could not see at all, as she was sitting at the other end of the room. Anyone as simply brought up and as shy as I was could only act very awkwardly the first time he was presented to a queen. When the queen asked me something, my reply was so confused and faint that she certainly did not understand a word of it, and no one was happier than I when I was back again at my hotel. The remuneration was considerable, but as I also played on the same evening in the Ludwigsburg Museum, where I received 8 gulden, I returned again to Stuttgart very happy. Best of all, the queen was an English princess and she had a letter of recommendation written for me with England in view, which I later received.

I now also hoped to play before the king, but was unable to achieve this honor, although I had taken all the steps which were required. As much as this annoyed me, I now believe that it was good for me; for if I had been successful in playing at the court in Stuttgart, I would have been in danger of becoming overconfident. I recalled the promise that I had made to my uncle and, as it was near the Christmas season, when bakeries have a great deal to do, it was easy now to obtain work for a few months. I worked at Murschel's bakery for two months and was well paid. I much preferred it there to Lüneburg and I learned much more, as I worked all day in the bakery. But scarcely was I at my job for two days when invitations began to arrive for private gatherings where I should be heard. My employer, a very benevolent man, permitted me these extra earnings gladly and was even pleased whenever a servant came to ask for me. I received 2 to 4 kronenthaler for an evening and as I was well paid at the baker's, aside from having free room and board, I earned a good sum of money in these two months. My present circumstances were so pleasant that it was really not right to leave them, especially because my employer wanted to keep me on longer. But various articles were now appearing in the newspapers about my playing and poets were writing verses about my Jew's harp—so I was not to be held back any longer. I firmly decided to make a musical career with my Jew's harp and not yield before any difficulties. At the same time, I decided to live in the simplest possible manner so that even in the worst case my money would not be exhausted. How far I deceived myself in this last point the reader will learn later.

On 3 January 1825, I said a final farewell to the bakery and wandered on foot up the Tübinger path, where the view of the fine city of Stuttgart put me in the most wistful mood. I later experienced much goodness in various cities, but the two months that I lived then in Stuttgart belong to the happiest of my life. For I found there sympathetic people who not only recognized my talent, but who also accepted me and showed me every possible kindness. In particular, however, I am still to this day obliged to these men because they did not let themselves be deterred by my position as a baker from promoting me as an artist. The many kindnesses which I enjoyed in Stuttgart not only aroused the feeling of gratitude in me, but also strengthened my trust in God and man. On one thing, however, I was firmly determined: not to abandon myself to overconfidence, regardless of my success, but to live simply and moderately. Yes, my desire to assert myself as an artist was so great and my decision to return to baking only in the most extreme emergency was so firm that I spent only three kreuzer on the whole journey from Stuttgart to Tübingen.

Because I had many friends among the students in Tübingen who staunchly supported me, it was not difficult to organize a concert. In this concert, for the first time, I played the Jew's harp with a guitar accompaniment, the latter played by Dr. Silcher. The concert was very well attended and I returned to Stuttgart with 36 guilders profit. I now went to Heidelberg, where I arranged a concert with the help of some students. Although there had been a large concert two days before mine, at which Herr Haitzinger sang and which was extraordinarily well attended, I still earned 30 guilders. Some of this was spent, however, because I did not succeed in giving a concert in Mannheim.

I now wanted to go to Frankfurt, but Herr Strauss, the conductor, advised me to go to Switzerland because of the many small wealthy towns there, because every city had a musical society and, finally, because so many rich families lived there who could engage me for an evening. He also asserted that my travels on foot would be taken less exception to there than elsewhere. As I had never seen Switzerland, I quickly made up my mind and traveled back to Stuttgart in order to inform my friends and patrons of my plan. It was generally approved and in less than eight days I had fifty letters of recommendation, the majority of which—and the most important—were from Privy Councilor Kaufmann, who had formerly been an envoy in Switzerland.

On 3 February 1825, I left Stuttgart for the third time and the next evening came to Hechingen. There happened to be a court concert taking place, at which I had the honor to play and for which I received 4 kronenthaler. From there I traveled on foot by way of Rottweil, Villingen, and Donaueschingen. I spent some very pleasant days there among the artists, one of whom was the conductor Kalliwoda. Unfortunately, the prince was away, but as I had letters of recommendation to his sister, she invited me to play. The princess was also there and I received 6 kronenthaler from her and letters under her hand and seal for Switzerland. I then went to Freiburg im Breisgau. I could not give a concert there because another artist had arrived before me. I played, however, at several private gatherings and in the theater, where the director gave me 6 kronenthaler. From all these small receipts I always saved something, since I traveled on foot and lived extremely simply. I now went quickly to Basel in two days. I was immediately told that I could not give a concert there because several benefit concerts were scheduled in succession. But I played at many private gatherings and managed to acquire 2 louis d'or in fourteen days. From there I went to Aarau, where I gave a concert which was very well attended, as well as two other concerts which I gave in Zopfingen and Lenzburg. In Aarau, the famous Zschokke invited me to dinner and was very friendly to me. I did not play in Baden, but that city will always remain in my memory because a dentist there wanted to extract one of my teeth and after he had tormented me frightfully for fifteen minutes, the tooth broke off at the root, which was later completely extracted by a dentist in Geneva. I now went to Zürich.

In Stuttgart I had already received many letter for this city, and as I had asked for letters to Zürich wherever I had given concerts, I had collected so many that I was assured of a good success here. There existed a musical society whose members were mostly of the upper classes and whose director was Herr von Blumenthal. As I had brought letters of recommendation to several of the most important members and to the music director, a meeting of the committee members was immediately organized to decide where I was to play. It was unanimously agreed that the society should give a concert for me. I was required to submit a list of the pieces which I wanted to play and I was told that in the meantime I could visit some smaller towns in the vicinity while the society was arranging my concert. I gave only two concerts in Winterthur and St. Gallen, but these turned out so badly that I quickly returned to Zürich in order to await my concert. A beautiful day enticed me to the Rigi, where I gave a concert and recovered my travel expenses. This concert occurred in a remarkable manner.

One of the Zürich gentlemen to whom I had brought a letter arrived just before me on the Rigi, where I met him. He was tremendously sorry that he could not hear me, whereupon I told him that I had my Jew's harp with me and that it would be my pleasure to play something for him. Afterward, at dinner, this gentleman made such a fuss over my playing that the guests unanimously requested that I play in the sitting room and that an entrance fee be charged.

The entrance fee was set at 24 kreuzer and the whole group of twenty-six people came. This little concert gave me a great deal of pleasure because it was the first time that something of the kind had ever occurred up there and because I now knew that I could earn something even on the highest mountains where no other artist would venture.

I returned to Zürich in the happiest mood and my concert occurred shortly thereafter. It turned out exceptionally brilliantly and the acclaim was unprecedented. The next day a servant brought me 10 louis d'or as the net profit of the concert. I had never earned so much money with so little effort at one time, and it was no wonder that the thought of going to Paris was reawakened in me. I made a plan to go to Lausanne in order to learn French, and from there to travel to Paris. This was quickly accomplished and I arrived in Lausanne at the beginning of June with 30 louis d'or. I found lodgings with a baker, took French lessons with one of the best teachers and studied well, so that in four months I spoke French decently. I now had the idea of taking up another instrument, besides my Jew's harp, on which I could later give lessons. I chose the guitar, which I had already learned in my youth. Although I played the violin ten times better than the guitar, the latter seemed more suitable to me because it was a woman's instrument. I made good progress on this instrument too and I was very happy indeed that after two months I already had a guitar student. In Lausanne, I could have had things as easy as in Stuttgart: I could have worked in a bakery during the day and played at gatherings in the evening. It was perhaps a mistake that I did not do this, only first of all I had no more desire for the bakery; secondly, my present clothes were no longer suitable for that; thirdly, it would have hindered my studies. I also had the feeling then that I would be happier as a musician living on bread and water than as a baker with the finest delicacies. I was later obliged to undergo the test of bread and water in reality, but cannot recall that it made me particularly happy.

I did not manage to give a concert in Lausanne, but earned a few louis d'or by playing at private gatherings. The most important thing that happened to me there was that I made the acquaintance of a Herr Stockhausen from Paris. This man heard me and held out hopes to me that I could accomplish something with my instrument in Paris. He gave me his card and promised that he would support me with advice and action in Paris. The reader will learn later how faithfully this gentleman kept his promise.

On 2 November I left Lausanne and wanted to try and earn something in Geneva, but after a stay of eight days I scarcely recovered my travel costs. It went the same way in Lyon, where I stayed for several weeks without being able to give a single concert. I was told everywhere that in order to succeed in giving a concert in a French city, it was absolutely necessary to have played to acclaim in Paris. I realized that quite well and now traveled directly from Lyon to Paris, where I arrived on 2 December at ten in the evening. My whole capital consisted of 250 francs. Directly the next morning I went out in order to orientate myself somewhat. The colossal spectacle and the terrible noise on the streets robbed me of any confidence in my little Jew's harp, and instead of paying visits, I ran around the whole day to acquaint myself with the streets and to accustom myself to the frightful din. I lived in the Hotel de Piemont, rue Ste.-Anne, and rented a room on the third floor for 30 francs per month.

As I was already in mortal fear the first day that I might be unsuccessful there, I made up my mind to live as simply as possible. My breakfast consisted of milk and bread; my lunch, of a small piece of meat with vegetables; and I ate nothing in the evening.

On the second day I paid only one visit—to Herr Stockhausen, who received me in a very friendly manner and advised me about everything that I had to do. On the third day I began to submit my letters of recommendation. My way took me across a boulevard, where it happened that a street cleaner wanted to shake his broom free of dirt: he struck it against a tree and the whole load splashed onto me. There I stood in the middle of the street, covered in filth, my new glacé gloves completely ruined, and jeered at besides. This was a hard blow for me and I went home to dry and change my clothes. Due to the great distances involved, I was only able to deliver three letters the next day, and it took a whole week before I was able to submit them all. I mentioned everywhere that I did not intend to give a concert, but to play at private gatherings; I soon learned, however, that it was not the custom in Paris to pay artists for performing at gatherings and that artists of the first rank played for nothing. I hoped, though, that an exception would be made for my Jew's harp as something totally new, but as I did not yet have a reputation, I had to accustom myself to playing for nothing beforehand. There were certainly many families, especially those to whom I had brought letters of recommendation, with whom that was possible, but no one wanted to be the first to pay me; instead, everyone promised to recommend me. In addition, I had to have a new suit made in order to appear respectable, and now I saw with terror that my small amount of money was dwindling away. The morning milk had to be stopped and was replaced with water; for lunch I ate a few cheap little fish with bread and salt. I was able to hold out for another couple of weeks on this miserable, meagre food. But, unfortunately, even this means did not help, for my money was finally exhausted before I had earned a single kreuzer, and while my playing was being admired in the leading salons of Paris, I almost died of hunger. There was nothing left for me to do but seek out a friend, which I did, however, only after not having eaten anything at all for two days. The friend to whom I described my wretched condition in a letter was Herr Stockhausen, whom I had met in Lausanne, and the result indicated that I had chosen the right man; for it was he who brought me out of this misery and it is he whom I have to thank for everything that I am now.

As soon as he had read my letter, he came to me and brought me money, while scolding me thoroughly for not having revealed my sorry state to him before. He also invited me immediately to eat with him. From that moment on I did nothing without him. At first he had the idea of going to those people to whom I had been recommended by letter and for whom I had played without payment, in order to inform them of my wretched state. This would have been a sure method of obtaining enough money for me to be able to return to Germany. The next day, however, he said that he wanted to spare me that humiliation before trying something else. He suggested that I support myself for a while by copying music, by means of which, if I were diligent, I could earn 3 francs a day which would be sufficient for my existence. During this time he would try to accomplish something for me through his students and my patrons. This plan was completely successful. Stockhausen immediately gave me some music to copy and the next morning I was writing it out at my little table. I was now tranquil and could return to my milk and small piece of meat. In the meantime, my benefactor worked on my behalf. He was a very popular harp teacher and composer, and his wife was an excellent singer who later made a great fortune in England through her talent. His students were mostly wealthy people of the upper class. He introduced me to all of these and there was scarcely an evening when I did not play at a gathering. A card was now printed on which I announced that my fee for playing at private parties was 40 francs. I brought this card to all the families to whom I had been recommended and Stockhausen gave the card to those of his students who he knew could pay me. As several very favorable articles about my playing now appeared in the newspapers, the paid soirées increased to the point that after four weeks I was able to give up copying music.

My friend and rescuer now planned that I should, after all, give a concert, so that those families for whom I had played without payment would have the opportunity to be of service to me. The day was appointed, but difficulties of every kind began to arise, in that several singers who had promised to participate free in my concert tried to rid themselves of the obligation by various excuses. I had to run around every day for almost three weeks, partly to place tickets, partly to bring the artists together for rehearsal; and if I had not had my friend Stockhausen, the concert might not have taken place at all. Best of all, during these three weeks more than two hundred tickets were sold in advance, and I also obtained many paid soirées, some among English families now as well. I was also introduced to the composers Rossini and Paer, both of whom expressed themselves exceptionally favorably about my playing. The latter introduced me to the Duc d'Orléans (afterward King Louis Philippe), who sent me 100 francs and later ordered twenty-five tickets to my concert. Rossini recommended me for several soirées where I received 50 francs.

The day finally arrived when my concert took place and I was anxious to know what effect my little instrument would make in the large hall. I was concerned that if the hall were too full, the quiet so necessary for my playing would be distrubed. Fortunately, not more than four hundred people came, all of whom had seats, so that no disturbance occurred. The concert was a decided success; the audience heard better than I expected: even in the duet for harp and Jew's harp, the latter was heard because Herr Stockhausen took pains to play very softly. Most of the newspapers expressed themselves favorably about my playing and only a few made jokes about it, which, however, did me more good than harm. This concert brought me, after deducting all costs, 1,400 francs; and as my reputation was now made, I obtained many more paid soirées. My requirements, however, also increased. I spent 300 francs to have clothes made for myself and, as a souvenir of this concert, I bought a ring with five diamonds, because I was advised that this belonged to the career of an artist. I also resolved now to apply myself particularly to playing the guitar in addition to the Jew's harp, and to this end I bought a guitar and many scores. I did not have a guitar teacher, but by a fortunate circumstances, two distinguished guitarists lived in my hotel and I had the opportunity to hear them both every day; one of them, Herr Horetzky, was a remarkable virtuoso, which was of great benefit to me, and my progress on this instrument was very considerable.

I now decided to go to London and wanted only to wait until I had played before the Duchess de Berry. This occurred on 14 April 1826 through Paer's recommendation. The latter wrote me a note that two other artists would also play: a flutist and a blind guitarist. When I arrived in the Tuilleries, the others were already there, for which I was scolded by Paer, although we still had to wait another hour because the king, who was honoring this soirée with his presence, took so long to appear. Scarcely had His Majesty entered than we were also admitted.

The ladies and gentlemen sat at scattered tables and we were placed in a corner where a piano stood. I was very tired and as there happened to be a chair near me, I sat down. I had been sitting for barely half a minute when the conductor nudged me with a remark that one must not sit in front of the king. I shot up like an arrow. Finally the command came to play and I had to begin. My playing pleased everyone except the flutist. He could not understand how such an insignificant instrument could be permitted before the court. After me, he played variations on the flute, but the king did not take any notice. The guitarist produced more of an effect, and both had finished, I was obliged to play again. I now played my "Trompetenwalz," whereupon the flutist wanted to start again. He was not admitted again, however, as the duchess now sang in aria. Immediately afterwards, she spoke a few words with me and we were dismissed.

The flutist repeated everywhere that I had been vulgar enough to play a waltz before the court; but what he did not say was that everyone had enjoyed this waltz, especially the king, who had smiled and nodded at me during it. After I had received my 200 francs, I left the same evening for London.

I was very sorry to leave Paris, and my days there are among the most important of my life. By listening daily to the greatest artists of Paris, I became an artist myself. In five months I rose from the deepest misery to the highest stage of my profession, and I actually laid the groundwork there for my future prosperity. But my wants now rose, in that I occasionally permitted myself an enjoyment. For the many gatherings I needed a great deal in the way of clothes, linen, gloves, carriage rides, and numerous other small things; briefly, my expenses increased with my reputation. Thus it happened that despite my large earnings, I remained comparatively poor in Paris, and after I had paid for my place on the mail-coach to London, I was left with only 800 francs. On 24 April, at four in the afternoon, I left Paris and arrived the next morning at six in Calais, where I remained until ten; at two I reached Dover by the steamboat. There, I was practically torn to pieces by the porters and hired servants until I finally found one who spoke French and who took care of my things. My trunk was brought to the customs, where I had to pay £1.10s.; my outlay for the porters and other expenses was another 10s., so that I had spent 24 gulden in one hour. This was a difficult beginning and I was worried that I would have the same experience in London that I had had at the start in Paris. The closer we came to London, the greater my anxiety became. I had taken a few English lessons in Paris, but could not speak one word, which increased my anxiety, so that I arrived in London in a miserable mood. The trunks were unloaded and set down, and now everyone looked after his own. With great difficulty, I made someone understand that I wanted a coachman, and in a few minutes I was at Gerodie's Hotel. It was seven in the morning and as no one was yet awake who spoke French, I had to wait half an hour until I could obtain a room. Unpacking and brushing my clothes took until noon, and I went out only around four in the afternoon. My first visit was to Herr Volker, the present cantonal councilor in Herbrook in Rheinthal. He went with me immediately to look for private lodgings, and the next morning at nine I was installed in a room at a tailor's establishment in Oxford Street. My rent was £1.00 per week. This seemed an enormous sum to me, but I was told that a respectable apartment was necessary in order to do business with the upper classes in London, so I was obliged to take the plunge, as I had letters to the highest personages. My money had now dwindled to 330 gulden and I found it necessary to organize my mode of life so simply that I would be able to hold out for as long as possible. Unfortunately, the families to whom I had letters lived very far from each other, so I had to hire a servant for five days who charged £1. The letter to Princess Auguste, which I had received from the queen in Ludwigsburg, I submitted through the Württemberg ambassador, who attached his card and particularly told the servant from whom the letter had come.

Count von Mandelsloh was generally the person who proved most useful with advice and action, and if I had not had this man as a patron, I would have left after two weeks.

Of all the families to whom I had letters, Princess Auguste was the only who sent for me and before whom I first played. But as no one was there except the Duke of Sussex, the evening brought me less benefit than I had promised myself. I received £5 and was served with a supper. On the same evening I played in another house where, however, the gentleman paid me only £2. This gathering was so noisy that my Jew's harp made scarcely any effect, for which reason the master of the house also thought that £2 was enough for music which no one heard. I was glad, though, that I had at least earned something, more indeed than I had spent in the ten days since my arrival in London. As Herr Volker, who also did a great deal for me, had introduced me to several journalists, articles immediately appeared in the newspapers which also added that I had already played before the Princess Auguste.

After this, I received several invitations to the first houses of the land, but as there were large, noisy gatherings everywhere, no one could hear anything: I was fobbed off with a couple of pounds and the engagements stopped again as quickly as they had begun. I was now almost in despair. My playing was greatly enjoyed at small gatherings, but these were not paid. I complained of my plight to Count von Mandelsloh, who comforted and encouraged me. Although he recommended me everywhere he went, he could not arrange for people at small gatherings to pay me as they did in Paris, and I saw to my horror that my money was diminishing. Had I been able to decide to hold out to the last heller, things would have gone better finally, but I did not want to venture this, and as the climate also did not suit me, I quickly resolved to return to Germany before my money was completely consumed, and chose the city of Hamburg as my next objective.

I packed my trunk and had already ordered a coach for six o'clock to take me to the place from where a boat was leaving the next morning, when at five-thirty an elderly gentleman entered my room together with a servant he had with him. He said that he had read several articles in the newspaper about my playing and wished to hear me, to which I replied that I was on the point of leaving for Hamburg, because everything had gone wrong for me in London. At the same time, I told him that I had played before Princess Auguste and, in general, mentioned something about the course of my career. He became more and more interested and asked me most particularly to unpack my Jew's harp and play for him. As I still had another half hour, I did so with pleasure. How great was my astonishment when, after the first piece, he cried out that I must under no circumstances leave! He placed £1 on the table, gave me his card and asked me to come to him the next day at eleven.

It was the Duke of Gordon.

Who could have been happier than I was now! For although I did not like London at all and I had already accustomed myself to the thought that I might perhaps, with the help of my Jew's harp, establish myself as a music teacher in Hamburg, on the other hand it was difficult to withdraw in disgrace after having come to London with so many hopes and such a great reputation. Everything was to change now. At precisely eleven the next morning, I found myself in the duke's apartment. My guitar, which the duke had arranged to be brought, lay on the table, and a few minutes later the duchess entered the room, and I was obliged to play. First Jew's harp, then guitar. After each piece, a great many questions were asked of me, especially how I had come to bring such an insignificant instrument to such perfection. The duchess was a kind lady of refined sensitivity, a benefactress to the poor and unfortunate; the duke also possessed these qualities, and every artist who has had the honor to play in this house will surely always remember the kind and benevolent condescension of both of them. The duke was my rescuer from distress, my benefactor and, with the exception of my friend Stockhausen, no one contributed more to my happiness than the Duke and Duchess of Gordon. As they are both dead, I will keep them forever in kind memory. The duke gave me £5 for my playing that morning, and in the next three weeks I played five times at his house and received £3 each time. Each occasion was after a dinner, and he always asked me to sit down and partake of the dessert. The reader may well imagine how this and the champagne tasted to me.

The high personages who dined with him soon noticed that I was a particular protégé of the duke's, which was of great benefit to me, in that I now played frequently at small gatherings and was well paid.

Before the duke left London, he recommended me especially to General Sir Andrew Bernard and asked him most particularly to recommend me to King George IV. After I had paid three or four visits to the general, I received a note one morning at eight that the king wished to hear me and that the general would call for me at four. He arrived in a carriage and we traveled to Windsor by the special mail. I was installed in a royal hotel and in the evening was called for by a royal coach, as the king did not live at Windsor, but in a villa nearby. When I left the coach, I gave the driver a pound sterling instead of a shilling, which I received back the next morning in exchange for a shilling.

Never in my life was I more tense and excited than on that evening, for it had always been my highest desire to play before the King of England, and now this was to be fulfilled.

At nine I found myself in the king's antechamber, but the music began only at ten. At first there was an overture by Händel, and the terrible din of the wind instruments made me very nervous because I thought of the weak sound of my own instrument. During the overture I glanced several times into the adjoining room where the king was sitting, but could not see anyone except Princess Esterhazy, who already knew me. When my turn came, the king wished me to play in his room, very close to him. As soon as I had made my bow, he began speaking German with me, and in the middle of the first piece he called out "Bravo!", which was repeated by the whole company. After the first piece, the king spoke with me again in German and desired me to move my small table nearer to him so that he could better see my method of handling the Jew's harp. When I played the second piece, I stood so close to the king that if a Jew's harp had fallen from my hand, it would have fallen on His Majesty's foot. After I had finished, the king spoke with me again, took one of my Jew's harps in his hand, looked it over from every side, and finally dismissed me.

There was now orchestral music again, followed by Herr Schulz from Vienna and his two sons, who played a trio for guitar and philhar-monica, and lastly, at the request of Prince Esterhazy, I played another waltz. When everything was over, the conductor Kramer grapsed my hand and, at the king's order, gave me £20. Schultz and I were then served a supper, where we drank Madeira from the king's cellar, and half an hour later we consumed a couple of bottles of Bordeaux with Kramer. The joy of having played before the King of England would really have been sufficient to daze me; but the Madeira and the Bordeaux also contributed their share, so that I did not know how I had come to be in bed. The next morning we went with the king's huntsman in ordinary to the park and saw the zoo, where the pouched animals that hop on two legs and carry their young in a pouch pleased us most. From there we went to see the king's boat and the gear with which he fished; after a short trip on the lake, we went back to breakfast, and at two o'clock we entered the carriage which brought us back to London.

I had been in my room scarcely half an hour when a coach came again to call for me, as the king, after I had gone, had expressed the desire to hear me again. It was the same as on the first day and for that reason I may omit a more detailed description.

I now ran to all the journalists whom I knew and to all my friends and patrons, in order to acquaint them with the honor I had enjoyed. It was immediately reported in five or six newspapers, and had the season not been so advanced, I would have become all the fashion. As it was, I obtained only a single soirée, where I took in the last £5. On the other hand, I had the honor to play in rapid succession before the brothers of the king—the Dukes of York, Cumberland, and Clarence (the next king), and before the Duchess of Kent (the mother of Queen Victoria), which brought me a further nice, tidy amount of travel money.

The season was now over: the wealthy went traveling or to a seaside resort. I was advised to go to Brighton, where part of the nobility had gone to take sea baths, only my heart drew me to Germany, and es-pecially to Lüneburg. For £4 a ship brought me to Hamburg in thirteen days (while now the trip can be made in a splendid steamship in two days for £2). Without delay, I went to Lüneburg, where I remained for ten weeks. There, I saw again the girl for whom I had nursed a silent love since my first sojourn. As I was loved in return, these ten weeks seemed to me like ten days, and with pain I saw the day approaching when I had to leave.

After my beloved and I had become secretly engaged and had sworn to be eternally faithful to each other, I set out for Heilbronn without having given a single concert anywhere. As my arrival had been announced in the newspapers, it was no wonder that a concert which I now gave was so filled that many people had to be turned away without having heard me. People came from the whole vicinity to hear me, and while two years earlier my concert had been attended by only twenty people, now there were 450.

It went the same way in Ulm, Tübingen, and several smaller cities. In Oehringen I played before the prince for the third time and was well rewarded by him, as well as by Duke Eugen. The court musicians remarked that I was not as shy this time as I had been two years before. I had previously made all these journeys on foot, but I could not do so any longer because I always had my guitar and many scores, as well as some books, with me in order not to interrupt my studies. All this cost a great deal of money; nevertheless, I was left with a much larger profit than two years earlier, when I had traveled on foot and played to empty benches. I now went to Stuttgart in the hope that I would happen to have the honor also to play before my king; but it could not be managed this time either, whereupon I canceled the concert which I had intended to give.

This was a mistake, and I am still convinced today that in Stuttgart, where I had begun my musical career and where I had so many friends and patrons, I would certainly have had a good concert.

With the beginning of the cold season I lost the desire to give further concerts in small cities and, as I planned in any case to return to London, I considered it better to remain in Heilbronn and prepare myself for this undertaking.

After a difficult farewell, I set out from Heilbronn on 20 January, in a frightful cold, and, in order to see my bride once more, traveled by way of Heidelberg, Frankfurt, Hanau, Kassel, Göttingen, and Lüneburg to Hamburg, where I boarded a ship and arrived in London on 28 April. On this journey I was less fortunate than before, in that almost everywhere, where I wanted to perform, I came at a bad time and was only able to give concerts in Heidelberg, Hanau, Göttingen, Celle, and Lüneburg, all of which, however, turned out indifferently. In Hannover I played before the Duke of Cambridge, who enjoyed my playing so much that he gave me letters for London under his hand and seal and recommended me to a number of private gatherings.

In Kassel, the conductor Spohr invited me to dinner and accompanied me in the evening at a gathering where I played his aria, "Rose, wie bist du reizend und mild" [Rose, how lovely and gentle you are]. I remained in Lüneburg for fourteen days; in Hamburg I did no business at all.

After arriving in London for the second time, on 28 April 1829, I still had 400 gulden from all the money that I had earned.

As I was obliged, in order to do business, to rent expensive lodgings again and spend a great deal at the outset for advertisements in the newspapers, I began to feel very frightened indeed already in the second week, for I noticed, unfortunately, that during my long absence I had been forgotten everywhere. The Duke of Gordon, upon whom I had counted most, was in Italy, and other high-ranking families to whom I had letters had also not as yet returned. I ran around day after day and only after three weeks was I successful in obtaining a paid engagement at a party. I later also played before the Duke of Cumberland, but on the whole my money continued to dwindle, and when the season was over and the families retired to the country, I had spent a considerable portion of my money. I decided nonetheless to hold out and to practice my guitar playing in order to establish myself afterward as a guitar teacher. I now took an inexpensive room and worked day and night, trusting in God. At this time I lived through four of the most difficult months of my life, and I sank from the highest pinacle of my fortune to the deepest misery. I felt how truly little fame and honor served to make men happy, and I also felt my wretchedness the more deeply because, due to my great reputation as an artist, I had considered it humiliating to return to being a baker. What still amazes me today, however, is that I had so much courage despite my distressing condition, and even more that I pursued my studies with so much love.

For I often sat over my guitar all day with a glass of water and a piece of bread, and my progress was so great that I was soon recognized as one of the finest guitarists in London. I also made considerable progress in thorough-bass and composition during those four months, and the number of compositions which I wrote during that time of torment was very large. I had no idea then that this would be of such great benefit to me afterward.

The winter had now come and I was obliged to take better lodgings, which made me very unhappy indeed, as I had only £8 left from all my money. Because I again had to pay £1 a week for rent, I now lived much more miserably than before and I scarcely dared to eat something every other day at noon, and even this was often interrupted by violent pains in my teeth. I found myself in this melancholy condition when Providence afflicted me with an even greater calamity. While I was eating, one of my teeth broke, which I needed to play the Jew's harp. This was the hardest blow that I had ever experienced, and if ever a person on earth was miserable and without any hope, that was I at this terrible moment. For a long time I had built my hopes on establishing myself as a guitar teacher with the help of my Jew's harp, and that my tooth had to break just now when I believed that I would be able to achieve this goal, I thought of then as the greatest misfortune that could have happened to me. The reader will soon learn, however, that Providence had imposed this fortunately brief test on me for my salvation.

The Duchess of Gordon had earlier recommended me to the famous dentist Cartwright, who had already extracted several of my teeth so skillfully that several hours later I could dine with him and even play a bit for him on the Jew's harp. I ran to this man now in my great distress and told him of my misfortune.

He examined the root and consoled me with the assurance that he would insert a false tooth by means of a gold pin, with which I would be able to play the Jew's harp for many years to come. On the same evening, he drilled a hole in the root, poured in a few drops of very sharp liquid and the next day, at one o'clock, placed the new tooth inside.

He invited me to dinner, as usual, and I now went home in order to lie down quietly, according to his instructions.

I did not feel any pain, but a great tension, which prevented me from playing the Jew's harp. This made me very miserable again. I went to him once more at six, however, to dine, and because I now despaired of ever playing the Jew's harp again, I was even more resolved to seek my salvation with the guitar. I took my guitar with me and played several pieces after dinner; this was the first time I played guitar at a gathering in London. My success was so great that already the next morning I had a student. She was a wealthy relative of the dentist and she and her husband both demonstrated great friendship for me later.

I now took fresh courage and ran to all the music publishers in order to offer my compositions for sale. As my name was already well known in all the music shops because of my Jew's harps and because I agreed to play my pieces everywhere, I was successful in selling a few manuscripts during the first couple of days. I now also went to all my friends and patrons, who were gradually returning to London, and told them— which was actually the case—that it was uncertain whether I would be able to play the Jew's harp again and that I had, for that reason, devoted myself completely to the guitar; and I entreated them all to recommend students to me.

At the same time, I offered to play without payment at parties, and I now found to my amazement that my guitar playing was considered to be of excellent, solid quality. As I played almost every day at gatherings, I soon obtained students; they also soon became my friends and patrons, and often invited me to dine with them, as well as recommending me as a guitar teacher to all their friends. By January I had so many students that I could not take any more.

Whether it was compassion or whether the students were especially pleased with my teaching I do not know; but I do know that I now found myself at the goal of all my desires, the more so as I was able to begin playing the Jew's harp again and in a short time could play as well with my false tooth as before.

When my students learned of this, they were all truly delighted, and I was obliged to play at gatherings every evening. I played gladly for my students without remuneration, and they recommended me for many paid soirées. I also played again at gatherings of scientists, which produced new articles in the newspapers. Through these, I once more received invitations from the highest nobility and, among others, had the honor to play a second time before the Duke of Cumberland and, especially, to speak with the greatly talented future King of Hannover.

I now found myself upon the highest level of my fortunes, thanks to the Providence which, after so much difficult testing, had placed me in a state which most corresponded to my nature and talents. I also recognized, however, that those tests were necessary; for if everything had gone from the beginning according to my desires, I would most likely have become, as mentioned earlier, overconfident, while I was grateful to my difficult tests and the sufferings that I had borne for many qualities which later contributed to my happiness, such as perseverance, moderation, thrift, avoidance of bad company, etc. How many young people have gone astray in big cities because things went too well for them from the beginning, and thus they came into bad company! Good fortune makes people too easily overconfident. For that reason it is salutary when Providence occasionally imposes difficult tests on us, so that we learn to bear good fortune better. Extended misfortune purifies man and gives him strength to bear his destiny; but extended good fortune not infrequently makes him soft and brings him to all sorts of delusions and vices. In addition, what at first seems like a great misfortune very often leads to happiness and vice versa, which everyone has undoubtedly learned for himself. For that reason, I would like to advise young people who read these lines that if they suffer a misfortune, they should not lose courage immediately or grumble about Providence, but rather accept that this misfortune was perhaps necessary to keep them from overconfidence.

I mentioned above how inexpressibly miserable I felt when, by the sudden breaking of a tooth, all my hopes seemed destroyed. Who would have believed then that this apparent misfortune was only to my benefit? But it was so. By breaking this tooth I obtained my first student and patroness through the dentist. This misfortune also brought me to serious reflection and resulted in my beginning to apply myself exclusively to the guitar, and ultimately to pursuing my career as a guitarist and guitar teacher with more diligence; but especially it kept me from misusing my present advantageous position and allowing myself to be seduced by dissipations.

When the London season was over, I could deposit a capital of £100 in the bank of England and I was now, in the opinion of all my friends, a made man. Unfortunately, I could not share this view, as I had become sickly on account of my many sufferings and privations and the mental strains associated with them.

My physician, who was at the same time my friend and student, had already told me earlier that London was not conducive to my health, and now the anxiety tormented me that a single extended illness could bring me once more into the deepest misery. Whoever has given lessons in London and knows the running around connected with them will not wonder at my concern, especially as the physician now seriously recommended that I leave the city for a while. It cost me a difficult struggle to give up my fine position; for although most of my students had already left London, I still had so many left that I could have lived well from them. It was only when my students themselves encouraged me to go to a resort in order to restore my health that I decided upon this difficult step. On the advice of my physician, I chose the bath at Cheltenham. I had scarcely arrived there and scarcely announced my arrival in the newspaper, when I received an invitation to play before the Duke of Wellington, who was then prime minister.

There I met Princess Esterhazy and learned that it was she whom I had to thank for the invitation, as she had told the duke that I had played before the king.

Immediately thereafter I received several invitations, as well as a few students for the guitar. My health also improved considerably, so that I felt strong enough to undertake the difficult business in London. After a stay of four months, I was just about to return to London when my faithful old friend and rescuer Stockhausen appeared. He had come to England with his wife in order to participate in concerts. A large concert took place in Cheltenham, at which Frau Stockhausen sang. The acclaim was so great that a second concert was scheduled and Stockhausen suggested that I should play a piece on the guitar at it. My departure was postponed and I practiced a single piece five to six hours a day for two weeks.

It was the first time that I played the guitar in public and for that reason I exerted myself to the utmost. My success, however, was also so extraordinary that I was obliged to play the piece twice. Stockhausen had gone to Bath between the first and second concerts in order to arrange a concert there, and when he returned he said immediately that he had now found a city for me which suited me completely and where I could establish myself as a guitar teacher. I traveled there right away and, on my first day, heard that there was no good guitar teacher, whereupon I immediately advertised in the newspaper that I would play at gatherings and give lessons on the guitar. As the city of Bath is the residence of many wealthy people, I did not lack for students here either; after four weeks I had so many of them that I quickly decided to stay there over the winter. I now wrote to my students in London that I would return only the following May, and received assurance from many of them that they would wait that long for me.

I began to condect my business with the greatest zeal, whereby the Jew's harp rendered me the greatest service, for through it I was more widely known in four weeks than would have been possible with the guitar in a whole year. I also received £2 for playing the Jew's harp and, as the number of my students gradually increased, I had earned so much money by May that I was able to deposit another £100. Had I not promised to return to London, I would certainly not have gone back, only as my students had waited for me so long, I left my fine business in Bath and arrived back in London at the end of May 1829. After a few weeks, however, my health deteriorated once more, and playing the Jew's harp at gatherings did not go as well as before. I therefore decided quickly that I would leave London and establish myself firmly in Bath as a guitar teacher. I was strengthened in this resolve by many letters which I received from my students in Bath, in which the wish was expressed that I might return to Bath.

As I was in the process, however, of publishing some of my compositions, I wrote to Bath that I would arrive there only at the end of July. Without my having anything to do with it, this was reported in the newspapers, which I took as evidence that my friends in that city continued to interest themselves in me. I took care of my publications as quickly as possible and had arranged my departure for the 10th of July when Providence tested me anew. I suddenly fell ill, so badly in fact that for several days my life was in jeopardy and I had to remain in bed for seven weeks.

This illness caused me double harm: I was unable to earn anything for eight weeks and, far more importantly, I arrived in Bath too late to teach in the schools. The physician allowed me to travel on 7 September and scarcely had I arrived in Bath when I felt much better, and in a few days I was again completely healthy.

I was less fortunate as far as my students were concerned. Some of them had waited for me, but others, who did not believe that I would return, had gone to another teacher, while most were still at resorts and on journeys. I had thus come to Bath too late for the schools and too early for the private families. But as everything in the world has two sides, so it was with my present circumstances. I heard that many teachers from Bath went twice a week to Bristol and Clifton to give lessons. I now thought of trying to do the same. Bristol is a mercantile city of 100,000 inhabitants and lies on a river suitable for shipping; Clifton, which lies much higher, is a sort of suburb of Bristol. Not only do the rich merchants of Bristol have their villas there, but several thousand wealthy people live there too and many private institutes exist. I went there for a few weeks and here, as well, my Jew's harp rendered me the greatest service; I very quickly obtained several guitar students. I decided to give instruction at Clifton twice a week, and returned to Bath, where some more students had registered. From now on business between Bath and Clifton became better from day to day. In order, however, to render my position more secure, I began to give lessons in German and found a few students in Bristol for this as well. As I still continued to play at gatherings in the evening, I derived great advantage thereby and I was soon convinced that Bath and Clifton were far better places for me than London.

Until now I had had the fixed idea that I could make my fortune far more quickly in London than in any other city because I had made my way up to the highest circles with my Jew's harp and because London offered the greatest field for my compositions. But as the air there, the mode of life, and especially the late hours were harmful to my health, I was constantly struggling with myself about whether to leave London or hold out there. My last illness and the great losses which followed it brought all these uncertainties to an end once and for all: I learned to realize that health is a far higher good than fame and money. It was now much easier to decide on the choice of Bath as my permanent residence and to give up completely the idea of later returning to London. The reader sees here again how unfathomable are the ways of God and how little cause we have to grumble about our destiny, and how much better it would be if we could bear it with patience. A person seldom has the strength to subordinate his passions and desires to necessity, and from that stems the constant dissatisfaction with our destiny which makes people so unhappy.

I had considered that illness to be a great misfortune and even began to despair of Providence because so many of my wishes were destroyed; it was only later that I saw it had all been for the best.

My business now continued in an orderly fashion for several years, and, as I always lived moderately, my fortune gradually increased. In September 1833 cholera suddenly and unexpectedly struck Bristol, occurring so violently that often eighty people died of it in one day. Clifton was spared from the disease, only its inhabitants were in constant fear and most of the families fled. I still went, as before, twice a week to

Clifton, but obtained very few students. In Bath, too, it went badly with lessons, and those families that were still in the country delayed their return because they feared that the cholera would also spread to Bath. One of my families went so far as to stop lessons with me out of fear that I might bring the cholera into their house.

My business now went very badly, and when things did not improve until October, I quickly decided on a final attempt to see whether I could make my fortune more rapidly with my Jew's harp than by giving lessons. As my students approved of the plan, they all gave me letters of recommendation, and because I had long ago received an invitation from my patron, the Duke of Gordon, I wrote to him that I was now able to come. I received a reply by return of post that he would expect me with pleasure on one of several days that he mentioned, whereupon I set out on 10 October 1833.

The first place I tried was Cheltenham, where I did good business because I was already known. From there I went to Liverpool, where I gave twelve concerts, but these were so badly attended for the most part that after a stay of six weeks I barely recovered my costs. I now traveled in a terrible cold to Edinburgh, where I arrived at ten o'clock in such a terrible storm that in alighting from the coach my hat flew away and I had to run with the greatest exertion for five minutes before I was able to retrieve it. It is strange that I was often able to bear small unpleasantnesses less well than great misfortune, for when I arrived at the hotel I was in such a miserable mood that I ardently wished that I were back in Bath. Less unpleasant and almost funny was the little adventure that I experienced that night. After I had been lying in bed for a while and could not become warm by any means, I got up again in order to put all of my coats and other clothes on the bed. When this too did not help, I got up once more and wanted to see whether pressure would be of use, so I placed not only my trunk, but also a drawer from my commode on the bed. Under this pressure I finally became warm and fell asleep. The next morning, when the boots came into the room and saw this barricade, he made an indescribably comic face. This was caused by repressed laughter, whereby, as everyone knows, each person has his own manner. Only when I myself laughed did he venture to laugh with me and understood the reason for the barricade. Whether the boots told the other guests, I did not learn, but at breakfast it seemed to me that several people put their heads together and glanced at me.

After I had paid a few visits in Edinburgh and several newspapers had made known my arrival in Scotland and my intention eventually to give some concerts there, I traveled directly to Gordon Castle, where my noble patron, the duke, called for me at the mail in order to accompany me to his castle. There, I had just enough time to dress, after which I was brought at six o'clock to the duchess's drawing room; she immediately realized that the duke had wished to give her pleasure on her birthday by my playing the Jew's harp and guitar. She was very pleased to see me again and a quarter of an hour later I was sitting near the duke at a table large enough for eighty places, where my frozen limbs, especially after the champagne, soon thawed again.

In the evening I played several pieces on the Jew's harp and guitar to great acclaim, so that I promised myself an encouraging success from my concerts in Scotland. I remained in this house for three weeks which I will never forget; overwhelmed with kindness, I left the castle on 3 January 1834 to give my first concert in Aberdeen, which was quite well attended.

From there I went to Edinburgh, where I remained for several months. I rented a hall for six evenings and listed the six concerts on one placard, but almost all of them were indifferently attended, and I saw that Scotland was not a profitable place for my Jew's harp. I allowed myself to be led astray, however, by the flattering reviews of my playing which were carried by almost all the newspapers, and announced another six concerts. But these too, with the exception of the last one, were poorly attended, so that I would never have recovered my costs if I had not had some letters of recommendation from the duchess to several of the highest families in the vicinity of Edinburgh, whereby a number of additional considerable honoraria accrued to me.

In order to console me over my limited success, many of my friends now stated that my concerts all over England would have gone better if I had begun in London. I readily believed this, as people in general readily believe what they hope and wish. I traveled in the greatest haste to London and rented a salon in Hannover [sic] Square Rooms, where I announced six concerts, as I had done in Edinburgh. But as it rained a great deal in London during this time and as there were many other artists in London, these concerts too were not very well attended. Only the last one was extraordinarily filled because my noble patron, the duke, who had come to London in the meantime, took this concert especially under his protection and honored it with his presence in a large company. The great success and acclaim I received that day gave me fresh courage and I now rented—as an absolutely final attempt—a small hall in Regent Street for a month. I advertised on small and large placards that I could be heard playing the Jew's harp all month from three until four o'clock every day. This speculation was also unsuccessful, however, and instead of earning a great deal of money, as I had hoped, I was in the unfortunate situation of having to spend part of the money I had earned earlier. In addition, I had incessant pain in my teeth, which brought me almost to despair and, finally, to make my unhappiness complete, I suffered remorse that I had been so foolish as to give up such a fine business as I had had in Bath. The only benefit which accrued from these many small concerts was that they increased my reputation also as a guitarist, which was later of use to me in various ways, in that I received a far higher price for both my lessons and my manuscripts than I had before. I had also ensured, through the distribution of free tickets, that my concerts were never completely unattended. And as all the newspapers continued to describe my playing as extraordinary, my last hope remained that I would be able very quickly to earn greater returns in the provincial cities; in this I was not disappointed. I first went to Cheltenham, where I did very good business, as also in the other small towns of the vicinity. From there I went to Bath and Clifton, where I gave several concerts which brought me a great deal of money. I was thinking that I could yet make my fortune with the Jew's harp when I was suddenly stricken with a new misfortune, the greatest I had ever experienced. The root of that tooth where my false tooth was fixed began to become inflamed and caused me such terrible pain that it became almost impossible for me to play the Jew's harp; I often suffered the most indescribable pain while my audience was listening with the greatest pleasure to my playing. Now, however, my last upper tooth broke and the dentists declared that both roots would have to be removed and that for the present there could be no question of inserting false teeth.

In despair over my melancholy fate, I quickly traveled to London in order to consult a dentist there, but he too stated that I had to give up the Jew's harp for a long time. I now felt inexpressibly unhappy that I was obliged to relinquish such a propitiously begun career so suddenly in the midst of my good fortune. All the more so because the wonderful goal, for which I had endured so much suffering and want, seemed so near; and I had already flattered myself that Providence had seen fit to reward me by my final success for the great patience with which I had borne years of suffering. But He who placed upon me this new and most difficult test at the same time gave me the strength to bear my lot, and after I had surrendered for a few days to the deepest anguish, I pulled myself together and found, upon reflection, that my condition was not so bleak as I had at first imagined. I had lost my best source of income, but I still had the hope that I could feed a family without my Jew's harp too. For I had made a great many friends in a wealthy city, who now demonstrated the warmest sympathy over my misfortune, and if it had not been June, when all the rich families went to the country, I would certainly have had a large number of students for both guitar and German language. I also had the happiness of being free of the horrible pain in my teeth and had to recognize humbly the wise dispensation of

Providence in afflicting me with these pains before I lost all my teeth. In any case, the loss of my teeth would have been more difficult for me if I had not had any pain beforehand.

As it happened, it was more possible for me to bear my misfortune because the loss of my teeth was also the end of the excruciating pains. Whoever has had an incessant violent toothache will surely excuse the fact that I have dwelt on this condition at such length.

Together with the idea of firmly establishing myself now in Bath came the longing to be united with the girl who, with such matchless love, had remained faithful to me for eight years and whose image had often floated before me, guarding me from many temptations. I imparted this decision to my friends and former students, and when I found that all of them without exception approved of it, I traveled full of hope to Heilbronn, in order to obtain my mother's blessing, and from there to Lüneburg, where I was united with my beloved bride. On 30 August, four days after the wedding, we arrived in Bath. But how great was my amazement when I learned immediately after our arrival that during my absence two new teachers had established themselves in Bath: a young elegant Italian for the guitar and a very talented German teacher! This news was like a thunderbolt for me. If I had still had my Jew's harp, the competition would not have been so keen for me; but in this case our state was an extremely sorry one, and what increased my misfortune was the fact that I had given my bride hope of a good living and now it appeared as though I had deceived her.

In addition, I was reproached for being guilty myself for everything because I had remained in Germany too long and many of my students believed that I would not return. Fortunately, my wife not only did not reproach me, but reassured me that she had no pretensions, that she kept house as simply as possible and that she would share my privations with loving self-denial. Whoever has a wife like that should never despair in any condition of life. We now struggled for five months with many privations and, in order to utilize my great amount of free time as well as possible, I wrote at that time my German grammar for Englishmen, which has gone through seven editions until now and which was later of enormous use to me.

After the grammar was finished and I still had only a few students, I again went more to Clifton; but there too the new guitar teacher had already played several times and had made some friends. For the time being, nothing remained for me to do but wait patiently in the hope that the Italian would bring the guitar into full fashion and that this would also benefit me later. In any event, his presence was good for me, in that I had to exert myself to the utmost in order to resist the double competition. Unfortunately, I conceived the idea of inventing an improved

guitar, which I called "octina" because it had eight strings. With immense difficulty and an expenditure of more than a 1,000 gulden, I
finally managed this, but had to give it up after selling six instruments
because in the meantime the Italian had left and now, at the end of the
first year, I was fully established as a guitar teacher and did not need a
second instrument. Thus, the competition, instead of harming me, did
me a great deal of good. The same thing happened with the German
teacher, who also left Bath several years afterward, for without him my
grammar, which was of such use to me later, might never have appeared. Both these aspects of competition, then, which I first considered
such a misfortune, contributed to my happiness. My business improved
from year to year and, as I had the good fortune to have a thrifty wife,
we were able to return after fifteen years with a sizable fortune to my
homeland, where we arrived on 27 August 1847 with our three lovable
children and settled in my native city of Heilbronn.

My musical career actually ends here, as far as it is suitable to communicate it to the public, for instead of constant change and excitement, a
quiet family life now occurred. I bought some land, built a house, and
planned on leading a very tranquil life. With the French revolution of
spring 1848, all my hopes were again destroyed. The great upheaval
which this period caused in the social conditions of Germany also had
the worst possible consequences for me. I returned to my native land
with the idea of enjoying in peace the fruits of my exertions of twenty
years, and now, instead, was obliged to live for years in constant anxiety
and uneasiness, which was increased by the fear of again losing part of
my hard-earned fortune; the thought that to become poor is worse than
to be poor was constantly before my mind. I felt now, for the first time,
that he who seeks happiness in the accumulation of earthly possessions
and worldly pleasures, instead of in the improvement of his mind and
spirit, deceives himself enormously. Since then, twenty-five years have
slipped by, during which time I have had many bitter experiences.
These, however, are not for the public; so I close my little book with
some good advice to those who are in a position or are tempted to give
up a business prematurely in order to devote themselves to private life.
    Those who have a good business and are used to increasing their
fortune should beware of giving up the same prematurely in order to
retire. Living on one's means is not as easy as many believe and the
longed-for rest is seldom achieved. Reality is also almost always different
from the conceptions which our imagination creates. One person com-
plains about boredom and takes up gambling and other vices; another
speculates on the stock market and loses his fortune in that way.
    The major drawback of living on one's means, however, is without

doubt that the idle and comfortable life it entails acts as a bad example for children and increases the difficulty of their upbringing considerably. It is also generally known that possession of a thing does not make people happy and that the labor involved in gaining an object is more satisfying than the possession itself.

DESCRIPTION OF THE JEW'S HARP

The Jew's harp is made completely of iron. This instrument, several centimeters in diameter large, is horseshoe-shaped. In the middle is fixed a flexible steel tongue which is moved by the hand. The little instrument is placed between the teeth and, while it is held fast by the thumb, second, and fourth fingers, the tongue is struck with the third finger; by breathing, tones are produced which maintain their very fine harmonics by means of the iron spring. Every Jew's harp has only one fundamental tone.

Eulenstein played using two Jew's harps at the same time. Another sixteen Jew's harps lay on a table in front of him; these he changed with lightning speed in order to increase the extent of the scale or to change key. It is a pity that this completely original music will never again be heard; for only a "genius" can bring virtuosity to this insignificant instrument, and today every minor talent easily obtains a regular musical education on any string or wind instrument, whereby there is no need to lose one's teeth—without which the whole art of Jew's harp playing is lost. Eulenstein was truly the last in his art and for that reason alone he should not be forgotten.

Pieter Brueghel the Elder: "The Peddler Pillaged by Monkeys." 1556–57. At *lower right,* note the box of Jew's harps.

Retail Dealers for Jew's Harps

THE FINEST JEW'S harps available today are sold under the name "Virtuoso Jawharp". These instruments have been made by generations of the same Austrian family since 1620. They are still completely hand-made of blue iron and spring steel, and they yield a superb tone. They are made in three sizes: small, medium and large, but the medium size is the most flexible for ordinary purposes; the large size has a wonderful resonance, but tends to have less range than the medium. The sole American importer of these instruments has had useful and inexpensive plastic cases made to protect the Jew's harps from being damaged. For information on prices, interested readers may write to:

Virtuoso Jawharps
278-A Meeting Street
Charleston, SC 29401

Lamellate bamboo Jew's harps are fairly readily available from one reliable source in the Philippines. The instruments are very well-made and attractively carved, but vary considerably in musical potential. They are not expensive, so readers who would like to try this form of the Jew's harp are advised to purchase at least four—on the average, one will probably be adequate for playing purposes. For current prices (which include airmail shipping), write to:

Silahis Arts & Artifacts
P.O. Box 178
Makati, Metro Manila
Philippines

Select Bibliography

AS MENTIONED IN THE introduction to this anthology, comparatively little scholarly research on the Jew's harp has been accomplished within the last 150 years. During the past two and a half decades, however, this trend has been gradually reversing itself and several very important studies, especially in the area of acoustics and classification have been published.

The most obvious evidence of increased interest in the instrument is to be found in the new editions of standard works of musical reference. John Wright, one of the most outstanding of contemporary performers on and scholars of the Jew's harp has contributed excellent articles to both *The New Grove Dictionary of Music and Musicians* (London: Macmillan, 1980) and *The New Grove Dictionary of Musical Instruments* (London and New York: Macmillan, 1984). Essentially the article in the latter work is an expanded version of that in the former. Wright's articles, which include good bibliographies, are far more comprehensive than the article on the Jew's harp by F. W. Galpin which appeared in the fifth edition of *Grove's Dictionary of Music and Musicians* (London: Macmillan, 1954), an article, moreover, that had no bibliography at all.

Given the space limitations of the work, Anthony Baines's article on the Jew's harp in *The New Oxford Companion to Music* (Oxford and New York: Oxford University Press, 1983), represents an improvement in some respects over the unsigned article published in the tenth edition of *The Oxford Companion to Music* (London: Oxford University Press, 1970), although the new article omits some interesting data to be found in the earlier one.

Among the older reference works, the most reliable account of the Jew's harp is to be found in Curt Sachs's *The History of Musical Instruments* (New York: W. W. Norton, 1940). In view of Sachs's long-standing interest in the Jew's harp, it is perhaps not surprising that he devotes a relatively large amount of space (about two pages in all) to discussions of the instrument.

One of the most valuable sources for information on the non-Western varieties of the Jew's harp is *Ancient and Oriental Music,* edited by Egon Wellesz (London: Oxford University Press, 1957), the first volume of a series designed to replace *The Oxford History of Music.* This work contains reliable data on the Jew's harp in a number of cultures, particularly in Southeast Asia and Oceania, including material on playing techniques and the use of the instrument in courting.

In contrast to the generally positive changes that have been made with regard to coverage of the Jew's harp in works of music reference, there has been a negative trend evident in general reference works. As an example, the concise entry under "Jew's harp" in the eleventh edition of *The Encyclopedia Brittanica* (London and New York, 1911) contains substantial information, most of which has been omitted from recent editions, where the Jew's harp is given only a few, not very illuminating lines.

Unfortunately, none of the standard works of musical reference have entries for any of the eighteenth- and nineteenth-century Jew's harp virtuosi, with the exception of Eulenstein, who appears in both *Grove's Dictionary* and *The New Grove Dictionary*. Eulenstein's inclusion is no doubt due to the fact that he performed extensively in England and, during his stay there, a small pamphlet was published about his life.

If the Jew's harp were to achieve sudden prominence in the musical world as a result of the virtuosity of some gifted individual sufficiently fascinated by the instrument to devote his talents to it, there would obviously be a great deal more interest aroused in the Jew's harp in musicological circles than is the case at the present time. This hypothesis is not as unlikely as it may seem: witness the immense popularity achieved in recent years by Gheorghe Zamfir, the remarkable panpipe virtuoso, especially in Europe. In the author's personal experience, it was impossible to find a panpipe in Germany in 1972—music-store employees looked blank at the mention of the instrument. Yet seven years later, the musical instrument shops had an extraordinary range of panpipes in all sizes, materials, and price ranges; instruction books for the instrument were available, and a number of German musicologists were beginning to take a great interest in doing research on it. All this was the result of the talents of one individual. Unless and until a phenomenon of this type occurs, it is doubtful that the Jew's harp will excite very much more interest in the future than it has in the past twenty years or so.

A glance at the bibliography below will be sufficient to indicate that, at least until the appearance of the journal *VIM*, most of the scholarship on the Jew's harp has been accomplished in non-English–speaking countries, albeit some articles were published in English. Unfortunately, however, practically all those who have written on the subject, with the exception of Ernst Emsheimer, have completely ignored the highly informative work in Russian that has been appearing in Soviet journals over the last few years. In an effort to make these articles accessible, the present author has translated several of them, very kindly sent to him by Ivan Alekseyev, for inclusion in *VIM*, and it is to be hoped that in the future, account will be taken of the increasing work done on the Jew's harp in the USSR.

The present bibliography is limited to publications dealing exclusively with one or more aspects of the Jew's harp or, in the case of books, to those where a separate chapter or section is devoted to the instrument. More specialized references are to be found in the bibliography appended to Dournon-Taurelle and Wright's *Les guimbardes du Musée de l'Homme*, as well as in the bibliography at the end of Klier's article in the present anthology. The discography has also been restricted to recordings consisting entirely or primarily of Jew's harp performances. Excellent detailed discographies, which include recordings where perhaps only one or two cuts contain Jew's harp pieces, have appeared in the first two issues of *VIM*.

Journal

VIM (*Vierundzwanzigsteljahrsschrift der Internationalen Maultrommelvirtuosen-genossenschaft*). The only periodical source for information—scholarly and practical—on the Jew's harp. Despite the fanciful German title, the contents of the journal are in English (or else have English summaries). Editor: Professor Frederick Crane, 930 Talwrn Court, Iowa City, IA 52240.

Books and Articles

Adkins, C. J. "Investigation of the Sound-producing Mechanism of the Jew's Harp." *Journal of the Acoustical Society of America* 55 (1974).

Bachmann, Brigitte. *Die Volksmusikinstrumente der Schweiz.* Zürich: Atlantis Musikbuch Verlag, 1981. Contains an excellent section on the Jew's harp in Switzerland.

Boone, Hubert. "Bijdrage tot de geschiedenis van de mondtrom, vornamelijk in de Nederland." *Brussels Museum of Musical Instruments Bulletin* 2 (1972).

Christen, H. "Schweizer Maultrommeln." *Volkschochschule* 27 (1958).

Crane, Frederick. "The Jew's Harp as an Aerophone." *Galpin Society Journal* 21 (1968).

Dobrobaba, P. "Slovno svetlyy ruchey." *Sotsialisticheskaya Yakutiya* (11 June 1980): 3. A very informative article on the use of the Jew's harp among the Yakut. Contains biographical information on Ivan Alekseyev. English translation by Leonard Fox in *VIM* 3 (1987).

Dournon-Taurelle, Geneviève. "La guimbarde." Doctoral thesis, Université de Paris X, 1975.

Dournon-Taurelle, Geneviève, and John Wright. *Les guimbardes du Musée de l'Homme.* Paris: Institute d'Ethnologie, 1978. A descriptive catalogue of the extensive Jew's harp collection in this well-known anthropological museum. There are excellent chapters on the acoustics, mechanics, technique, classification, typology, construction, and distribution of the Jew's harp, as well as a great many fine photographic illustrations of the instruments themselves and of Jew's harp players from many parts of the world.

Emsheimer, Ernst. "Über das Vorkommen und die Anwendungsart der Maultrommel in Sibirien und Zentralasien," *Ethos* (1941): 3–4.

———. "Maultrommeln in Sibirien und Zentralasien." In *Studia ethnomusicologica eurasiatica.* Stockholm: Musikhistoriska Museet, 1964. Contains invaluable material on the Jew's harp in these areas, much of it based on Soviet sources.

Galayskaya, R. "Vargan u narodov Sovetskogo Soyuza." In *Problemy muzykal'nogo fol'klora narodov SSSR: Stat'i i materialy.* Moscow: Izdatel'stvo "Muzyka," 1973. A comprehensive treatment of the Jew's harp in the Soviet Union. English translation by Leonard Fox in *VIM* 3 (1987).

Geiser, B. "Maultrommeln in der Schweiz," *Informationsbulletin des Schweizer Musikrats* 1 (1975).

Il'ina, L. G. "O prelomlenii traditsii yakutskogo fol'klora v 'Kontsertnoy improvizatsii dlya khomusa i simfonicheskogo orkestra' N. Berestova," *Tvorchestvo kompozitorov Sibiri (Voprosy muzikal'nogo yazyka i stilya),* Vypusk 1 (1983). An extensive tratment of the use of folk music in Berestov's "Concert Improvisations for Jew's Harp and Orchestra." English translation by Leonard Fox in *VIM* 3 (1987).

Klima, Josef. *Spielanleitung für die Maultrommel.* Munich: Musikverlag Josef Preissler, n.d. A brief self-tutor for the Jew's harp, with some information on the history and use of the instrument. Includes music (mostly German or specifically Bavarian).

Kunabaeva, A. "Zhivaya legenda," *Sotsialisticheskaya Yakutiya* (26 January 1986): 3. An informative article on the current status of Jew's harp performance in the Yakut ASSR. English translation by Leonard Fox in *VIM* 3 (1987).

Ledang, Ole Kai. "On the Acoustics and the Systematic Classification of the Jew's Harp," *Yearbook of the International Folk Music Council* 6 (1972). One of the most important articles to appear on the Jew's harp in the twentieth century.

Leipp, Emile. "La guimbarde," *Revue du Son* 126 (1963).

———. "Etude acoustique de la guimbarde," *Acoustica*, 13 (1963): 6.

———. "Un vocoder mecanique: la guimbarde," *Annales de Télécommunications* 18 (1963): 5–6.

———. "La guimbarde," *Bulletin du Groupe d'Acoustique Musicale* 25 (1967).

Li Hwei. "A Comparative Study of the Jew's Harps among the Aborigines of Formosa and East Asia," *Bulletin of the Institute of Ethnology, Academia Sinica* 1 (1956). In Chinese with English summary.

Meyer, W. "Von Maultrommeln, Flöten und Knochenschirren," *Studia instrumentorum musicae popularis* 5 (1977).

Meyer, W., and H. Oesch. "Maultrommelfunde in der Schweiz." In *Festschrift Arnold Geering zum 70. Geburtstag.* Bern, 1972.

Otruba, Gustav. "Die Maultrommeln und Ihre Erzeugung zu Molln: von der Zunft der Werkgenossenschaft," *Oberösterreichische Heimatblätter* 40: Heft 1 (1986). This work will undoubtedly remain the last word on the history of the Jew's harp makers' guild and the Jew's harp industry in Molln.

Rydbeck, Monica. "Maultrommeln in Funden aus dem schwedischen Mittelalter," *Res mediaevalis*, 1968.

Sachs, Curt. "Die Maultrommel: eine typologische Vorstudie," *Zeitschrift für Ethnologie* 19 (1917). The first systematic work on Jew's harp typology; still quite valuable.

Sevåg, Reidar. "Munnharpa," *Norsk Musikktidsskrift*, 3 (1971).

———. *Det Gjallar og det Laet.* Oslo: Det Norske Samlaget, 1973. Contains an extremely informative chapter on the Jew's harp with invaluable illustrations and photographs.

Vertkov, K., G. Blagodatov, and E. Yazovitskaya. *Atlas muzykal'nykh instrumentov narodov SSSR.* 2d ed. Moscow: Izdatel'stvo "Muzyka," 1975. Much material, including illustrations, on the Jew's harp in the Soviet Union. English translation of all Jew's harp sections by Leonard Fox in *VIM* 3 (1987).

Wagner, A. "Das 'Trumpi' und das Trumpi-Wappen," *Archives héraldiques suisses* 56 (1942).

Wright, John. "The Trump," *Folk Music Ballads and Songs*, n.s. 4 (1967).

———. "Another Look into the Organology of the Jew's Harp," *Brussels Museum of Musical Instruments Bulletin* 2 (1972).

Music

Albrechtsberger, Johann Georg. "Concertino in D for Jew's Harp, Mandora and Strings," published as *Musica Rinata* 21. Budapest, n.d. (Available from Musica Rara USA, 305 Bloomfield Avenue, Nutley, NJ 07110.)

———. "Concerto in F-dur für Maultrommel, Mandora und Streicher." Munich: Musikverlag Josef Preissler, n.d.

Discography

Albrechtsberger, Johann Georg. *Two Concertos for Jew's Harp and Mandora* (the concerti in E and F). Fritz Mayr, Jew's harp, Dieter Kirsch, mandora, and the

Münchener Kammerorchester conducted by Hans Stadlmair. Orfeo S-035821 A.

Alekseyev, Ivan. Six recordings on the Soviet "Melodiya" label. Numbers unavailable.

Calanduccio, Emanuele. *Die Maultrommel*. Gold Records 11 139.

Mayr, Fritz. *Mozart auf der Maultrommel*. Arias from Mozart operas arranged for Jew's harp with lute accompaniment by Dieter Kirsch. 45 rpm. Elite Special 17-880. (Available from Bairisches Volksmusikstuberl, Bräuhausstrasse 8, 8000 München 2, W. Germany.)

————, and Helmuth Mayr. *Volksmusik auf der Maultrommel*. Two 45 rpm recordings of Austrian and Bavarian folk music. Munich: Bairisches Volksmusikstuberl.

Oberallgäuer Maultrommeltrio. *Allgäuer Volksmusik auf der Maultrommel*. 45 rpm recording of Austrian folk music. MPA 2.011 EP.

Ruspoli, Mario. *Les guimbardes*. Paris: Vogue SLD 862.

Terry, Sonny. *Sonny Terry's New Sound: The Jawharp in Blues and Folk Music*. Folkways FS 3821.

Wright, John. *La guimbarde*. Includes a well-illustrated four-page essay on the Jew's harp. Paris: Le Chant du Monde LDX 74434.

————. *The Lark in the Clear Air: Irish Traditional Music Played on Small Instruments*. Many Jew's harp cuts, some together with Dave and Mike Wright. Topic 12TS230.

————. *John Wright Unaccompanied*. In addition to the Jew's harp, Wright also plays fiddle and harmonica. Topic 12TS348.

Index

Page references that appear in italics indicate illustrations.